The Irrational Consumer

The Irrational Consumer

Applying Behavioural Economics to Your
Business Strategy

ENRICO TREVISAN

GOWER

Published by
Gower Publishing Limited
Wey Court East
Union Road
Farnham
Surrey, GU9 7PT
England

Gower Publishing Company
110 Cherry Street
Suite 3-1
Burlington
VT 05401-3818
USA

www.gowerpublishing.com

Enrico Trevisan has asserted his moral right under the Copyright, Designs and Patents Act, 1988, to be identified as the author of this work.

Translated by John Paul Wilson

British Library Cataloguing in Publication Data
A catalogue record for this book is available from the British Library

ISBN: 978-1-4724-1344-4 (hbk)
ISBN: 978-1-4724-1345-1 (ebk – PDF
ISBN: 978-1-4724-1376-5 (ebk – ePUB)

Library of Congress Cataloging-in-Publication Data
Trevisan, Enrico.
  The irrational consumer : applying behavioural economics to your business strategy / by Enrico Trevisan.
    pages cm
Includes bibliographical references and index.
ISBN 978-1-4724-1344-4 (hardback) -- ISBN 978-1-4724-1345-1 (ebook) -- ISBN 978-1-4724-1376-5 (epub) 1. Consumer behavior. 2. Economics--Psychological aspects. I. Title.
HF5415.32.T74 2013
658.4'012--dc23

2013010233

MIX
Paper from
responsible sources
FSC® C013985

Printed in the United Kingdom by Henry Ling Limited,
at the Dorset Press, Dorchester, DT1 1HD

CONTENTS

LIST OF FIGURES

ABOUT THE AUTHOR

The author, a recognised expert in pricing and behavioural economics, is partner at Simon-Kucher & Partners, the world leader in pricing consulting.

Enrico Trevisan studied Political Science at the University of Turin. He has a master's degree in Business Research from the University of Munich and a PhD also from the University of Munich in Strategic Management and Consumer Theory with a focus on Behavioural Economics.

PREFACE

One of the principal novelties of behaviourist economics, born out of the works of Nobel prize-winner Daniel Kahneman, Amos Tversky and Richard Thaler in the '70s and '80s, was the abandoning of the concept of *homo oeconomicus* – that approach to economics which had seen the consumer as a powerful 'calculator', able rationally and selfishly to pursue objectives determined by personal and coherent preferences.

Studying the real but often irrational mechanisms that govern consumer choice, behavioural economics determines how a commercial proposition might be perceived by consumers, how this perception could be influenced by the structure of the offer and of the price proposed by the seller and how this phenomenon works independently of the needs and desires the consumer had before entering the real purchasing decisions.

The book aims to present some of the most important findings of behavioural economics and to highlight the resulting opportunities for up-to-date commercial strategies.

This is the first book entirely dedicated to the application of behavioural economics in business.

It presents a number of the most important findings in behavioural economics, analyses the effective decisional mechanisms of consumers and suggests concrete ideas and concepts in order to optimise the profit potential deriving from the exploitation of these factors. The topic dealt with is highly relevant and innovative and will have a strong impact on companies' profitability.

The text examines practical examples and applications of these behavioural mechanisms in business cases and empirical studies.

INTRODUCTION

The critical study of the theory of rational choice has fascinated me since my university days. Why we make certain decisions in certain circumstances, often defying common sense and our own intentions, has always been a fundamental question for me. While I have often acknowledged the importance of systems, of organizations and of collectives both in the economic and social spheres, it has always been my conviction that the correct analytical perspective will focus on the individual and the factors guiding his choice.

When I began to further explore this question in my working life and to research, in relation to pricing and commercial strategies – how buyers select products and what sacrifices they are prepared to make to obtain them – it was a natural step to connect these two worlds. This book is the fruit of the attempt to systematically and comprehensively unite the ideas I had explored as a student with the more recent notions emerging from my professional activities, within the framework of the discipline of behavioural economics.

Now, 30 years on, behavioural economics has accumulated a vast body of data concerning how people decide and, in particular, on the role played by the presentation and the articulation of the choices on offer. Although this has had repercussions for many areas of economics such as labour markets and the welfare economy, in the book I will limit myself to the conclusions of behaviourists relating to consumer choice, with particular reference to factors which influence the perceived value of a given product and the associated maximum buying price.

While classical consumer theory has always upheld that the factor guiding our choices is the utility of the 'pay-off' which we attribute to these choices, behavioural economics has instead focused attention on the fact that the pay-off itself is not linked in a coherent and substantive manner to the choices, but rather is influenced by the 'architecture' of these. When for example we must assess what price we are prepared to pay for a certain product, our decision is determined not only by the value we associate with that product, but also by our expectations or assumptions regarding what such a product 'should' cost. This can lead to situations where the same product at the same price can seem particularly good value or particularly expensive, simply according to the points of reference we use in making our assessment. Are we prepared to invest our money for a return of 3 per cent? It depends if we expected 2 per cent or 4 per cent. Are we disposed to invest 20 minutes of our time in order to obtain a discount of €5? It depends whether the discount relates to an item costing €20 or €150. Do we want to spend €50 for a book? It depends whether we consider it as an investment in our cultural and personal development, or whether it is simply for enjoyment.

There can be considerable variation in the representation and framing of a given choice, depending on the consumer's personal and innate cognitive processes. Equally, external factors within the pricing, product and sales strategy can also play a role. The aim of this book is precisely to show how and why the pricing, the nature of the product and the selling technique can influence the choices made by consumers. The experiments and the psychological mechanisms illustrated are thus all referred to a context of buying and selling, i.e. to situations where the choices and the situation referenced are uniquely related to phenomena arising from the evaluation, selection and utilization of commercial offers.

While the reading of a book can often amount to a monologue addressed by the writer to the reader, this is certainly not true of its composition, at least not in my case. Far from being the work of a single protagonist, a multitude of people have aided me to identify, articulate, organize and express the ideas contained in the text. First thanks should undoubtedly go to the three authors who have made the greatest contribution to the birth and development of behavioural economics: Daniel Kahneman, Richard Thaler and Amos Tversky. I first came across some of the key ideas formulated by these authors while I was writing my degree dissertation, but it was during the drafting of my doctoral thesis that I came to study their findings in depth. Fifteen years on, I am still fascinated by the precision, the elegance and the novelty of their work.

Three other authors have had a strong influence on my ideas regarding the behaviour of consumers, of group dynamics, and more generally of commercial, economic and governmental organizations: Jon Elster, Werner Kirsch and Hermann Simon. The works of Elster and Kirsch have been fundamental to establishing a bridge between the disciplines of political science, philosophy and sociology on the one hand, and the theory of rational choice and of the firm on the other, a connection running directly or indirectly throughout this whole book. The works of Simon have taught me the bulk of what I know today concerning pricing, marketing and commercial strategy. While I cannot be sure I have not misinterpreted, or misunderstood, the full import of their arguments, and must therefore take full responsibility for any errors or inaccuracies, nevertheless if it were not for these authors the book you have in your hands would not have existed or would have been quite different.

Equally heartfelt thanks must go to my team at Simon-Kucher & Partners. The writing of a book in tandem with a career in consultancy could rapidly become an impossible task without the support of a group of young and talented colleagues. In this regard, my warmest thanks go to Raffaele Brusco, Lorenzo Busca, Gianluca Corradi, Mauro Di Donato, Paolo Finotelli, Sonia Foltran, Peifeng Gao, Alberto Laratta, Cristina Liotta and Alessandro Maggioni for their useful comments and editing work. Further, I would like to thank them for on occasion having to manage without my close and direct involvement in their working activities in order to dedicate the necessary time and energies to the writing of this book. At the risk of repeating myself, I cannot over-emphasize the degree to which their ideas and encouragement have aided me in completing my task and more generally in finding the courage to undertake such a venture.

A special word of thanks must go to Alessandra Lanciotti. If sometimes the acuteness of her observations is not matched by a corresponding conviction in expressing them, all the time spent discussing key aspects of the book with her has been repaid with apposite, rigorous and extremely useful suggestions. While considering Socrates' maxim 'know that you do not know' generally to represent a useful moral and epistemological precept, in the case of Alessandra I am tempted to make an exception, reminding her that 'you don't know that you know'.

Last I would like to turn with enormous gratitude to my wife, Suscha. It is perhaps strange that in a book concerning the dynamics of choice, not even a paragraph was dedicated to the most important decision we face in our life, the person with whom we wish to spend it. In my case I have no doubt that none of the decision-making anomalies and singularities illustrated in the book played any role in the decision to marry Suscha, which was without doubt the most sensible decision I ever made. The many hours in the evenings or weekends stolen from my family to be dedicated to the book were always met with understanding, patience, good spirits and compassion. And at times when I was having problems with a particular idea or with getting into my stride, her intelligence and her fresh mind helped me to find a new, different and better path.

A final mention for little Sophia and Greta. It is always fascinating to contrast the spontaneity of children with the contrived thinking of adults, and to see how different is our irrationality from theirs. Dear girls, by the time you are old enough to read this book (if you ever do) you will have embraced the irrationality of grown-ups. This is a shame, for yours is better!

CHAPTER 1

THE LOSS OF RATIONALITY

One of the principal novelties of behaviourist economics, born out of the works of Daniel Kahneman, Amos Tversky and Richard Thaler in the '70s and '80s, was the abandoning of the concept of *homo oeconomicus* – i.e. the approach to economics which had viewed the consumer (or more generally the economic agent) as a powerful 'calculator', able rationally and selfishly to pursue objectives determined by personal and coherent preferences.

Leaving this anthropological conception behind them, the behaviourists redefined our view of mankind in two different directions. Firstly, they asserted that the manner in which people perceive and interpret reality is strongly influenced by heuristics – more or less conscious mental strategies of simplification and reorganization of the available information. Secondly, they affirmed the existence of specific situational mechanisms which push decision-makers towards choices which are irrational – neither coherent nor consistent and not optimal in terms of the conscious objectives which they had set themselves.

1.1 HEURISTICS

Let us examine the case of heuristics and the way in which we perceive decision-making problems. The factors which we need to identify and analyse in the moment of making a choice are varied and uncertain, being often related to the future or to contexts regarding which we have incomplete information. For example, when we have to decide which model of car to buy, one of the fundamental things we ask ourselves is whether a given car is safe and reliable. Part of our willingness to pay for the car derives precisely from our expectation of acquiring a vehicle which is solid and capable of running smoothly for many miles.

One of the cognitive strategies which the consumer uses in order to arrive at a satisfactory estimation of this reliability, while committing a minimum of resources, is what behaviourists refer to as 'availability'. By reference to this heuristic the consumer tends to make use of all the information which comes easily to mind, either because (s)he has heard it at first hand, for example in the context of a recent conversation, or perhaps through direct experience. Certainly the interested and attentive consumer will seek to accumulate a stock of data relating to the car which is as broad and as balanced as possible, by referring for example to objective external sources such as trade magazines or a motoring club; however, his mind will not evaluate the various types of information in a statistically valid way. Rather, he will – often without even being aware of it – tend to focus his attention on more easily memorable facts. Thus the frequency with which the car suffers from mechanical problems will be assessed, on the one hand, by reference to studies performed by the motoring club recording the number of calls for assistance received throughout the year for that make of car; but, on the other hand, equal or even greater weight will be given to the single anecdote heard over dinner from a neighbour describing, with a wealth of personal background details, the occasion when a specific problem arose, the trouble it caused and the costs incurred to resolve it.

From a purely statistical point of view, it makes no sense to put these two types of information on the same level, for the simple reason that the difference in sample size entails a completely different degree of representativeness and of reliability. Nevertheless, this type of distortion works when seen from the perspective of an economy of cognitive effort. Then, while over the course of evolutionary history the human mind has always been confronted with more or less direct experiences from which it has had somehow to learn in order to avoid repeating the same errors, the development of inductive statistical reasoning, together with the ability to collect information regarding single events or experiences in a systematic manner across space and time has been much more recent. The mind's capacity to perform these two types of cognitive operation is therefore very different, as is the effort required to do so. The use of the 'availability' strategy is therefore comprehensible from an evolutionary point of view. It remains irrational, however, from an economic standpoint, in that it makes use of information which is insufficient for the comprehensive assessment of the costs of safety and a related rational choice based on a specific driver.

1.2 THE ANCHOR EFFECT

Many other factors influence our ability to choose and to evaluate in a rational manner. Consider the phenomenon which is referred to in the technical literature by the term 'anchor effect'. Economic theory assumes that what is important in our decisions is the end result in terms of well-being or utility. For a given buying decision, for example, the key is the price we must pay, not what we have paid in the past. But this is not always so. In reality, in many situations it is the latter and not the former which determines our decision, because it constitutes a point of reference with regard to future occasions. In this case, the original price becomes an 'anchor' to which our judgement of later options is closely bound.

This was shown clearly in an experiment I organized recently involving a sample group of people potentially interested in opening a savings account. In it only 48 per cent of respondents who were offered a savings account yielding 3 per cent interest in place of 4 per cent on their existing account were inclined to accept. On the other hand, 84 per cent of respondents offered the option of passing from an interest rate of 1 per cent to 2 per cent indicated they would accept. From an economically rational standpoint, clearly it makes no sense that more people were inclined to accept a return of 2 per cent rather than 3 per cent. Evidently, the rate of return in itself is not the only factor affecting the decision, but also the difference compared to that obtained in the past. This past rate of return thus determines a point of reference ('anchor') in relation to which respondents evaluated the different options, which in the former case constituted a loss of 1 percentage point in the rate of return and in the latter case an equivalent gain. Obviously this 1 percentage point loss or gain played a decisive role for the majority, which was more important than the resulting interest rate obtained.

1.3 THE DEAL EFFECT

Another fundamental mechanism for understanding consumer behaviour is the so-called 'deal effect'. According to rational theory, the sacrifice the buyer is prepared to make in order to obtain a product – the price – depends on the value we associate with the possession and use of the product, and is influenced by the various alternatives available on the market which might avoid the need to make the sacrifice, as well as naturally on the question of whether the price is affordable for us. In short, we will buy the product if we like and/or need it, if it is better than any alternative and if we can afford it.

However, in many situations the acceptable cost depends less on these considerations than on the context or the manner in which the product is sold. In actual fact, it is the context which determines our willingness to spend our money, as much as the product in itself or the nature of the buying experience. When for example I asked a group of people to choose between a current account priced at €1 and a 'package' comprising a current account together with a credit card at €2.50, 59 per cent of respondents chose the package while 41 per cent opted for the current account alone. However, for a second group of respondents, the same options were offered together with a further option of buying the credit card alone for €2.50. In this case, 81 per cent chose the package while 17 per cent preferred the current account alone and the remaining 2 per cent the credit card.

From a point of view of rational choice, this substantial shift in preferences in favour of the package is inexplicable. In fact, in the second experiment the credit card offered separately was clearly a sub-optimal choice. Why buy a credit card at €2.50 when I could obtain it together with a current account at the same price?

Logically, apart from those (2 per cent in our study) who had absolutely no wish to acquire a current account – possibly to avoid administrative complications – 98 per cent of the sample did not opt for the card on its own. The fact of the card being offered separately nevertheless modified the distribution of preferences between the other groups.

What can have caused this shift in preferences? The simplest explanation is what Richard Thaler (1980) calls the deal effect. In the first study the two proposals could be compared only by reference to their content. In principle, it was difficult to determine whether the account alone or the package represented better value in that they involved distinct products at different prices. In the second case, the option of the credit card at €2.50 created a direct point of reference for the price of the package, which suddenly appeared to represent better value. In the specific context of the choice, the package appeared particularly interesting because it offered more than the card alone at the same price.

1.4 THE SEPARATION EFFECT

Another effect encountered in many purchasing situations is the so-called 'separation effect', i.e. the phenomenon whereby the very separation of the moment of payment from the moment of acquisition and enjoyment influences the buying decision and/or the effective usage of our purchase.

In this regard, classical economic theory assumes that the time delay between these two moments plays a role only in two cases: when the utility of a product now is greater than in the future, or when the potential buyer anticipates a change in the resources at his disposal during this interval. Very often, however, what is observed in practice is an influence deriving from this separation which goes beyond what might be expected in terms of capitalization or risk in relation to the product being acquired, or any possible changes in resources available.

Let us take the example of the credit card. The possibility of separating the moment of payment from the moment of acquisition of goods appears to increase expenditure to a degree which is not justified by the fact that payment is postponed – on average – by a month. Instead, it appears more plausible that consumers do not have the same awareness and hence 'memory' for purchases made by credit card as for those paid in cash. Field studies (Soman 2001) have effectively demonstrated that differences in behaviour deriving from the separation of the moment of payment from that of acquisition cannot be explained simply by reference to a high discounting function – i.e. by an excessive weight assigned to the present in comparison to the future. It is simpler and more realistic to conclude that this separation influences our assessment of utility function, increasing the positive value associated with the acquisition and diminishing the negative value associated with the payment.

1.5 THE CHOICE EFFECT

Let us turn now to the ability to choose. Classical rationalistic theory assumes the consumer is able to efficiently assess the characteristics of a product by investing a minimum of resources in order to obtain a maximum result. In this theory, the consumer will interrupt the selection process when (s)he judges that the additional (marginal) utility obtainable by further research effort does not match that obtainable by finding a superior product. This capacity to interrupt the process of selection at the appropriate moment makes it possible to achieve an optimal management of the complexity and multiplicity of potential alternatives provided by the market. This signifies that the more alternatives are available, the greater the chances of finding the best option. Among many options, the expected utility is greater than when fewer options are available. But this is not necessarily the case.

In some situations, the number of options represents a problem and not an opportunity for the consumer, who is unable to identify the most acceptable proposition precisely because the high number of possibilities precludes comprehensive evaluation, weighing and comparison. Iyengar and Leeper (2000), for example, have demonstrated that while a vast range of choice for a given product can stimulate the interest of consumers, this does not translate necessarily into a higher level of purchases. In the context of the classical AIDA schema (Attention, Interest, Desire, Action), variety can generate attention and interest but not necessarily the desire or the act of buying.

1.6 THE ENDOWMENT EFFECT

A further interesting mechanism is the 'endowment effect'. Classical economic theory assumes that direct costs (so-called 'out-of-pocket costs') are related in some way to opportunity costs or, in other words, that there is a link between the costs associated with doing or getting a certain thing or with not doing or getting it. Thus, in this view, when the price corresponds exactly to a value where the consumer will have a neutral orientation between buying and selling a given product, the fact of being a buyer or a seller should have no influence on the value of the product in question for the consumer. But this is not always so.

In reality, the value we ascribe to a product to be bought tends to be lower than the value associated with the same product once it is in our possession. Basically, our negative reaction associated with spending money in order to acquire an asset seem to outweigh the positive reaction generated by the proceeds of its sale, and likewise the loss of an asset in our possession in comparison with never having possessed it.

If someone offers us a reasonable sum to buy an old collection of VHS videos that we keep in the cellar it is possible that we will refuse. At the same time, it is extremely unlikely that we would be prepared now to pay the same sum in order to acquire these videocassettes. This phenomenon could be explained by a certain sentimental attachment to the objects in question. But if we consider the fact that these objects will probably remain closed in a box in the cellar for years, it may be easier to explain it by reference to the endowment effect. Spending money now in order to buy these videos would mean losing the money in order to obtain them. Likewise, selling them would mean losing them in order to obtain money.

In both cases, we would not accept the transaction because the negative reaction associated with losing something (whether money or videocassettes) is greater than the positive one associated with acquiring it. Even if the same sum of money or the same videocassettes are involved we would remain attached to one or the other according to the situation we started from. What determines our willingness to buy or sell is therefore not only the item/s in question, but also our role as buyers or sellers.

1.7 THE ACCOUNTING EFFECT

When we must decide whether to spend a certain sum in order to buy a certain object, another fundamental aspect influencing our decision is the way in which we categorize the object in relation to other past or future expenditure. Field studies (Tversky and Kahneman 1981) discovered for example that if, entering the cinema, I realize I have lost the ticket costing $10, I will probably not be inclined to reacquire it. If, however, on arriving at the ticket window, I realize that I have lost a $10 banknote, I will be less likely to forgo the movie.

This is because, contrary to classical theory of consumer behaviour, our decision is not directed towards an end-state of overall well-being determined by our decision, but simply an improvement or deterioration in relation to a much more context-related point of reference. In terms of overall well-being, the two scenarios are practically identical: will I go to the cinema in exchange for a reduction of $20 ($10 for the first ticket and $10 for the second ticket or $10 for the lost banknote and $10 for the ticket) in the total sum of my wealth?

What drives the consumer towards a different reaction to the two situations is the fact that in the first case he attributes the cost of the two tickets to the same category of expenditure (cinema), making it appear relatively costly. In the second case, the loss of the banknote is not directly associated with the visit to the cinema but is 'entered' under a different category of expenditure. Spending \$20 to go to the cinema might seem extravagant and so it is better to do without the second ticket – i.e. the movie. This decision need not, however, be determined necessarily by budget constraints or, more generally, reluctance to spend \$20 that evening. The explanation lies rather in the fact of having a dual point of reference in the second case – \$10 in relation to the cinema and \$10 in relation to some indeterminate overall budget for petty weekend cash expenditure. The sacrifice associated with the cinema in the first case is therefore much greater than in the second case. Here the loss of the banknote is effectively registered under a different heading and will not greatly influence my decision on whether to go to the cinema or not. The categorization of expenditure in one way rather than in another can therefore have an immense bearing on my 'willingness' to spend, and this categorization is often completely arbitrary, inconsistent and highly influenced by the manner in which the choices are conceived.

1.8 THE SELF-CONTROL EFFECT

The lack of coherence in economic choices determined by the manner in which these are conceived or by how the information is processed is not the only source of irrationality in the consumer. Often there is an anomalous variation in preferences based on the placement in time of the 'payoff'.

The key tool for the incorporation of the time factor into our choices under the theory of rational choice is the discounted-utility model and the related exponential discounting function developed by Nobel prize-winning economist Paul Samuelson in 1937. The idea underlying this approach is that present value of the 'utility' which we expect from an asset available today is consistently superior to the present value of the utility we would expect to obtain from the same asset if it were available tomorrow. In reality there are two different time factors which influence our choices and can often cause a reversal in our preferences.

The first is the time elapsing between the availability of one asset and that of another. The second is the interval between the moment when we determine our preferences between alternative assets and that in which the assets actually become available. Whilst the former dimension is included in the discounted-utility model, the latter is not, even though in many cases this is the decisive aspect in our choices.

For example, when we seek to acquire a health 'asset' by deciding on Friday to start eating less fatty foods and carbohydrates from next week, but then on Monday we succumb to the temptation of eating unhealthy food – with probable consequent feelings of guilt on Tuesday – we are faced with a case where the second of the time factors mentioned above has determined our choice. The period of time required in order for the results of a healthy diet to be seen must in fact be measured in months, if not years. The difference between the two choices, however, is the distance between the decisive moments: days in the case of choosing the diet and moments in the case of choosing the food. So, when on Friday I decide to start a diet on Monday, I know that from that moment on the results of the diet will be visible in months. When then on Monday I disobey myself and start to eat unhealthy food, it still holds true that the results of this will be visible only in the long run. The only difference between Friday and Monday is the time lapse between the moment I plan to follow the diet and the moment I must actually start to do so.

In the same way, when with the arrival of autumn we resolve to start saving for Christmas presents and therefore to reduce the number of CDs we normally purchase, only to find ourselves on the following Saturday afternoon buying them anyway, and again possibly feeling remorse the moment we leave the shop, what has determined our behaviour is the distance between the immediate payoff (the CDs) and the moment of choice between CDs and Christmas presents, rather than the distance in time between the two alternative payoffs (CDs now or Christmas presents in a few weeks).

This variation in preferences derives, however, not from any conscious awareness or from fresh circumstances which finally convince us that dieting or saving money is no longer necessary (i.e. changing our preferences in a stable manner) but rather represents a sort of rebellion against our own selves. Moving on from the moment in which we decided to make a sacrifice towards the moment of actually making it, it often happens that the willpower necessary to put our decision into practice is lacking, so causing us to fail to keep to our original plan. This desire to do something in the future, not doing it when the future has become present and then regretting it when the future has become past, may be represented as an unstable or hyperbolic future discounted-utility model which varies precisely according to the time lapse in relation to the first choice of options and not to then time lapse between the options themselves. Our discounting function is therefore not stable over time, but is strongly affected by the interval between assessment and action.

This instability often leads to irrational forms of behaviour, preventing the subject from obtaining the intended result, only to regret it afterwards. Given that many aspects of life are characterized by a temporal dimension – i.e. by situations in which an immediate sacrifice or investment are a necessary precondition for attaining future results (e.g. investments, studies and learning, non-smoking and non-drinking, etc.) this inconsistency and weakness constitutes a very serious problem of rational behaviour.

1.9 COMMERCIAL STRATEGIES

In order to formulate an effective commercial strategy, businesses need to give serious consideration to the types of phenomena presented above in order to assess their importance, applicability and effect in the context of specific commercial situations. By studying these kinds of mechanisms, companies will thus be better placed to understand how a given commercial proposal – for example a savings scheme – will be perceived by the consumer, as well as how this perception could be modified by other reference points introduced by the seller (i.e. alternative products offered) and how this phenomenon can operate in relation to real buying and consuming patterns

Two possible basic strategies could be followed: a more aggressive form of marketing by which companies could seek to exploit the consumer's limited rationality in order to influence his buying decisions for their own ends, or a form of paternalistic marketing by which they might aim to help the unwittingly irrational consumer to overcome his irrationality through an appropriate formulation and declination of the product, pricing and sales strategy. Without wishing to embark on a moral discussion of this, I believe that in the long run the paternalistic option will be more valuable, both for consumers and firms. The main goal of a private company should be generating profits, and I am not aware of a better way of doing this than by creating real value for its clients. Behavioural economics should be used to nudge consumers towards more valuable buying options, not to manipulate them for the sake of a short-term increase in sales. Using this knowledge to cheat clients would at the same time conflict with sentiments of fairness and trust and ultimately provoke a backlash in terms of protests and lost sales.

It is therefore essential that companies be aware and make use of this new knowledge in order to anticipate and/or prevent 'irrational' modes of behaviour. They should thus determine which elements effectively add value for the customer, in what context, and which communication strategies are appropriate. Last but not least, they will need to identify how much consumers are really ready to pay for the various components of a 'proposal' and to what extent this willingness can be exploited by using underestimated behavioural mechanisms. The aim of this book is to present some of the key discoveries of behavioural economics and to highlight the resulting opportunities for articulating a modern commercial strategy.

CHAPTER 2

A PASSION FOR DEALS

The price represents the sacrifice that a consumer must make in order gain possession of or access to a certain product or service. The paying, spending, outlay of money is generally unwelcome, because it prevents us using that money for other ends. In point of fact, often it is not so much the need to give up other alternatives which makes the spending of money unwelcome, but the idea of losing the money itself.

Think of the classic figure of Walt Disney's Uncle Scrooge, of his fabulous wealth and of the business acumen, together with the spirit of self-sacrifice, which have enabled him to accumulate that wealth. But what makes this character unique, both comic and tragic at the same time, is his limitless devotion to money and his absolute determination not to part with it. This is why for Uncle Scrooge – as for many of us – the payment needed in order to acquire a product takes an enormous effort, because it means doing without the money in itself.

Assessing the sacrifice which the price demands of the consumer is therefore related not only to the associated opportunity cost (what must I do without in order to acquire this item?), but also to the direct cost in terms of the loss of or separation from money (how much cash must I sacrifice in order to pay the price for the item?).

2.1 THE IMPACT OF 'FREE'

It is precisely this second type of sacrifice which appears best to explain the impact of 'free' in buying decisions. Normally, the distribution of preferences between alternative products tends to remain stable with a parallel price variation, where price differentials are unvaried in absolute terms. If we prefer a cashmere sweater costing €200 to a Merino wool one costing €150, normally we will maintain this preference when the sweaters are offered for €250 and €200 or for €150 and €100.

Certainly, a higher or a lower level of prices can have an impact on spending limits (budget constraints) or acceptable price thresholds, and thus on choice. So, for example, some consumers may think it inconceivable to pay more than €200 for a sweater of whatever type, while others may consider the offer of a cashmere sweater at less than €200 to represent very good value and thus decide to spend a little more than they had intended in order to acquire it. For a third group the reasoning may be exactly the opposite: a cashmere sweater at less than €200 cannot be good quality and therefore is better avoided. Having said this, within the limits – financial or psychological – represented by price thresholds, generally there is a certain consistency between preferences for alternative items and variations in price levels where the difference remains constant.

When, however, while maintaining a constant price difference, the cheaper option is presented at a price equivalent to zero, the distribution of preferences can be transformed. In moving to levels where one of the two products is free, the balance of sales now shifts decisively toward the zero-priced product in comparison to the more expensive one. This means that the volumes of the free product increase disproportionately while those of the positively priced product diminish. The trend in preferences and in demand shows a marked discontinuity which is even greater than that found when exceeding any possible price thresholds.

Ariely (2008) performed an interesting experiment in this regard, demonstrating precisely this type of mechanism. In the first phase of the study participants were offered the option of choosing between a quality praline priced at 15 cents and a mass-produced chocolate priced at 1 cent. Faced with this alternative, 73 per cent opted for the premium product while only 27 per cent chose the cheaper alternative. In the second phase of the experiment the same products were presented but the price of both was reduced by 1 cent, passing to 14 cents and 0 cents respectively. This small price change in absolute terms was sufficient to completely invert the pattern of preferences. As a result, preferences for the praline went from 73 per cent to 31 per cent of participants, while those for the mass-produced chocolate rose from 27 per cent to 69 per cent.

Obviously this type of change cannot be explained in terms of limits on available resources (i.e. budget constraints). In Western countries (the experiment was conducted with students from a prestigious North American private university) it is hard to imagine that a difference of 1 cent could modify so dramatically the borderline between those who can afford chocolate and those who cannot, or possibly who prefer to buy something else with the money saved.

As Ariely observes, this change in the pattern of demand is anomalous even from a cost/benefit point of view. If in the first experiment the difference between the utility of the handmade chocolate and the price of 15 cents was greater than the difference between the utility of the chocolate and the price of 1 cent for 73 per cent of the students, in the second experiment this difference should have remained the same in that the prices of both products had been lowered by an identical amount. However, if:

$$(U_p - P_p) > (U_c - P_c) \text{ but } (U_p - P_p - 1 \text{ cent}) < (U_c - P_c - 1 \text{ cent})$$

where U_p represents 'utility of the praline', P_p 'price of the praline', U_c 'utility of the mass-produced chocolate' and P_c 'price of the mass-produced chocolate', then the simplest and most convincing explanation seems to be that the fact of passing from a minimal price to a zero-price changes the whole nature of the transaction. An assessment in terms of the trade-off, i.e. the weighing up of what I obtain (in product terms) in exchange for what level of sacrifice (in money terms) now becomes superfluous. As we will see in Chapter 4 ('Spoilt for Choice'), the very fact of no longer having to perform this type of evaluation or calculation can move preferences in a given direction. This happens because zero-cost transactions are characterized by the absence of separation from or loss of money. The buyer is not obliged to give up anything. The decision to accept thus takes on an exclusively positive light, and the zero-priced product emerges a clear winner. There may be many reasons not to buy a product costing only a few cents, but practically none not to opt for one which costs nothing. The typical attitude is thus 'Why not, after all I have nothing to lose. Let's take it.'

Is a 'free' strategy always a good commercial strategy? Is a success in terms of sales volumes necessarily a success in terms of profits? The wager many companies are making when offering their products for free is that they will be able to acquire customers to whom they may then be able to sell other products or who might be induced to upgrade to products with a higher added value after having tried out the basic version. This naturally assumes that the other supplementary, complementary or premium products in the range are sufficiently attractive to bring about this shift.

Another objective associated with companies' use of this pricing strategy is to establish a broader client base. The size and nature of this client base could make it interesting to other companies as a prospective 'user-pool' of clients or as a target for advertising. In this regard a key role is played by the 'network effect', whereby a community of users reaches a sufficient size to become of interest to new members. Thus the Microsoft Windows operating system – integrated with no additional cost for the buyer in all new PCs – became progressively more attractive over the years thanks to the growth in the number of its users and hence the number of contacts with whom data could be exchanged without systems compatibility issues. Many of the products offered free by Google are comparable, as is the logic of the user community which underlies Facebook's business model. The aim is not to extract value directly by requiring a payment from the user, but rather to create a community which will attract advertising and selling opportunities aimed at third parties.

Cross-selling and up-selling potential on a big starting volume base together with network effects represent two key commercial advantages of the zero-pricing approach. But there are also great risks connected to this strategy. One of the biggest dangers is that the zero element 'pre-selects' a certain category of clients who are particularly motivated to spend as little as possible and who have limited financial means; such customers will be difficult to shift towards premium products and will offer limited scope for cross-selling. This type of strategy will further require of companies the deployment of considerable resources in organizational and marketing terms. For, while the initial sales potential is strongly influenced by the attractiveness of the zero element, where the pricing acts of itself to push the client towards acquiring the product, subsequent up-selling or cross-selling activities will generally require an additional contact with the client. This will imply marketing campaigns and the involvement of a sales team who must make contact with, cultivate and motivate the client, in a context where the initial product had a cost of zero and where the commitment felt by the customer to the product, to the supplier and to the brand was potentially non-existent.

The initial advantage of zero in terms of the attractiveness of the product can thus entail disadvantages in terms of customer selection and typology. This risk can further extend to the wrong influence of the client. The threat is that the zero-price mark can in fact become a sort of mental 'anchor', to which the consumer makes reference when assessing future prices. In an experiment performed recently I noted exactly this kind of phenomenon. I asked a sample of 155 people to indicate their preference between a basic current account with a monthly fee of €2 and a premium account with a monthly fee of €4. The majority of the sample, around 65 per cent, showed a preference for the premium product, while the remaining 35 per cent chose the basic one. In order to validate the results, I ran two counter-experiments with two distinct samples of 155 people. In the first experiment I again presented the choice between the two types of current account, but here both products were free of charge for the first year, while from the second year on the price would have been respectively €2 and €4. In the second experiment the choice was again between the same products, but in this case the monthly fee for the first year was €6 for both options. While in the first counter-experiment the percentage of people interested in the premium current account decreased from 65 per cent to 48 per cent, in the second the percentage increased from 65 per cent to 79 per cent, with a variation of 17 and 14 percentage points, respectively. Since the samples were broad and almost identical from a statistical point of view, the most reliable explanation for this shift in preferences is that the first-year price became the anchor for the prices of the following years, a fact that strongly influenced the willingness to pay. When people expected to obtain the product for free, a price of €4 for the following year would have been too expensive, so in many cases people preferred to choose the cheapest solution (€2). This is the reason behind the decrease in preferences for the premium product from 65 per cent to 48 per cent between the original experiment and the counter-experiment with a first-year price of zero. Instead when people's expectations were determined by a first-year price of €6, the price of €4 for the following year did not seem so excessive, and the number of people interested in the premium product rose from 65 per cent to 79 per cent.

It is interesting to note that these two experiments are essentially based on two very common commercial strategies. The first of these is 'try with no risk and you will be satisfied' while the second is 'if you buy my products and stay loyal, I will repay you with a significant saving'. The first strategy offers the advantage of minimizing customers' resistance to purchase, because it allows them to purchase a product without costs, even if only for the first year. This is the reason why this kind of approach has a big appeal for customers and therefore a great potential in terms of market volumes. The obvious disadvantage, however, is that, besides being unprofitable in the first year because these volumes are achieved with zero revenues, they are also likely to be scarcely profitable in the long run due to the way they were generated, which has strongly downgraded their pricing potential.

Many business sectors have experienced this kind of problem. When for example many Internet service providers began to offer email accounts and addresses free of charge a few years ago, they created an expectation on the part of clients regarding a 'fair' price which still persists today. While for the majority of consumers having access to an email address has now become extremely important, almost indispensable, their willingness to pay for the product is almost non-existent. There is value, but it can no longer be extracted.

Banks experienced a similar phenomenon when they started to offer online current accounts at zero cost. Ten years ago this strategy might have made sense given that the banks had to overcome substantial doubts in clients' minds regarding the security of online transactions as well as problems in introducing users to and familiarizing them with the use of the Internet in general and online banking in particular. These two factors have now more or less ceased to apply, and the convenience and the reliability of Internet banking constitute an important source of utility for consumers. Nonetheless, the zero-price 'anchor' remains deeply embedded in the minds of clients (as well as of many product managers) and imposing a tariff on this type of service remains extremely problematic. It is not, however, any lack of value in Internet banking which makes it hard to price it positively, but simply the expectations of customers who over the years have become accustomed to obtaining it free of charge.

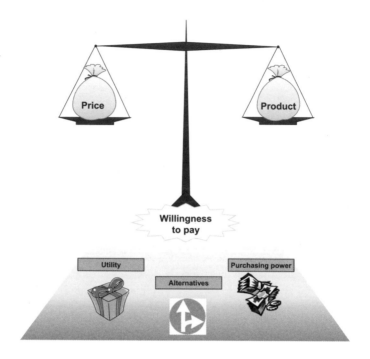

Figure 2.1   The deal effect: what is the rational consumer supposed to do?

2.2 TRANSACTION UTILITY

Having briefly analysed the impact of zero-pricing on the consumer's willingness to buy and to pay, let us now turn to a more normal market situation, i.e. when the 'free' strategy is not an option and in fact a sacrifice in terms of a price to be paid is asked of the potential buyer. As mentioned above, classical economic theory states that the sacrifice the purchaser is disposed to make depends on the value expected from the product plus other possible complementary value (utility). It can also be influenced by alternatives available on the market which might make it possible to avoid the sacrifice, and it is limited by the degree to which the purchaser's means enable him to bear the related direct and indirect costs (spending power associated with what economists term budget constraints).

Going back to the example of the sweaters, the consumer decides whether or not to purchase one according to the enjoyment expected from its use and/or possession, to the other sweaters (jackets, sweatshirts, etc.) which could be bought in its place and, lastly, to whether there are sufficient economic means to buy it (in simple terms, whether or not we can afford it). The combination of these factors determines in the potential buyer a specific willingness to buy. If this willingness is greater than the cost of the product, the purchase will take place, otherwise it will not. The price thus represents a variable which is appraised with reference to the product (acquisition utility), to alternative products available (purchasing alternatives) and to available means (budget constraints). From the consumer's point of view therefore the product is a generator of value, while the price is a detractor.

In many situations, however, our willingness to spend depends not on the product but rather on the context (sometimes imaginary) of its sale. Let us examine the interesting experiment performed by Thaler (1985) in relation to a bather's willingness to spend for a cold beer. The participants were asked to imagine the following scenario: 'Imagine you are relaxing on the beach on a hot summer's day and you feel like a beer. A friend, who is going to make a call, offers to buy you one from (a) a small grocery store or (b) a fancy resort hotel. What price are you prepared to pay for the beer in these two situations?'. From the point of view of the theory of rational choice, the responses should have been identical in the two situations. After all, the product was identical (same expected utility), obtained in the same manner (delivered by the friend), in the presence of the same alternatives (drinking nothing) and paid for out of the same resources (the personal budget constraints of the participant). The prices quoted were, however, widely different. In the case of the hotel, the average price indicated was $2.65, while for the store this became $1.50.

This experiment demonstrates that it is often the 'source' (the seller) of the product that influences the price we consider appropriate. There is not necessarily any difference in terms of 'enjoyment of the buying experience' or 'persuasiveness of the sales pitch'. In the experiment, in fact, the respondents were not physically placed in front of an elegant setting or a persuasive salesman, but simply given a theoretical idea of where the beer was sold. The simple fact of envisaging a luxury hotel rather than a rundown store modified expectations in regard to the reference price, and it was precisely this that engendered a different willingness to spend. It is thus not only the product or the service that generates value, but also the setting in which it is sold. The setting in turn is defined not only by an objective buying experience, but also through the imagination or a mental projection (Fig. 2.2).

There are situations in which it is truly the price as such which influences the desirability of a product. In this case the price acts as a *generator* or *detractor* of value and not only as an *extractor* of value in the classical sense. According to the price we expected – the reference price – the client assesses the price requested positively or negatively (other factors such as utility, possible alternatives and purchasing power being equal). There are two typical manifestations of this phenomenon. The first case is when the price requested is lower than we expected. Here the price itself generates utility in accordance with the principle we refer to as the 'good deal' factor. The surprise of being able to acquire the item desired at a good, and unexpected, price, will strongly influence our perception of the product. Even if it is the same as before, what adds value now is the cheap price. The second case consists of the opposite phenomenon: the price asked is higher than we expected. In this scenario the price itself generates disutility in line with the principle we refer to as the 'bad deal' factor (Fig. 2.3).

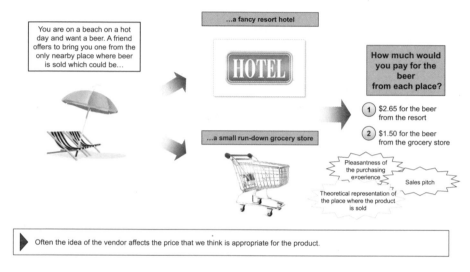

Often the idea of the vendor affects the price that we think is appropriate for the product.

Figure 2.2   The deal effect: who sells the product?

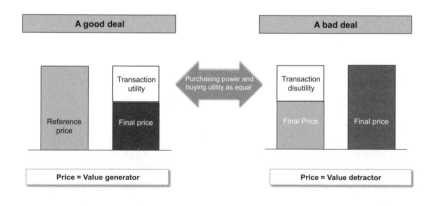

Customers obtain two types of utility from buying a product: the **purchasing utility** and **transaction utility**. The latter measures the perceived value of the deal within a specific buying context and can strongly influence the purchase decision.

Figure 2.3   The deal effect: what is my reference price?

To explain this phenomenon we need to clarify the concept of acquisition utility mentioned above, on the basis that the consumer in actual fact obtains two types of utility in buying something: *acquisition utility* which measures the value of the item in relation to its price and is basically equivalent to the classical consumer surplus; and a second type of utility, which Thaler terms *transaction utility* and which measures the perceived value of the deal. It is defined as the difference between the real price requested in the market and the reference price for the product, i.e. the price the consumer expected to pay.

This distinction in relation to the concept of utility has two important ramifications in the context of the market. Many products are bought because they constitute a good deal, i.e. they have a positive transaction utility, even if their acquisition utility is slight or even negative. An important example of this phenomenon is a special form of the so-called impulse purchase. The consumer is not really attracted to the item being bought, but rather to the terms on which he is able to buy it at that moment. Take the example of certain types of promotion in large stores or hypermarkets where baskets are filled with products which are not necessarily useful or which will never be consumed by the 'use before' date. How many times do we find our shopping trolley filled with items which we had no intention of buying and for which we will find little or no use, simply because they were offered on terms which we perceive as particularly advantageous?

A converse example is when we do not buy products because we consider them 'unjustifiably expensive'. In these cases the acquisition utility may even be considered positive, but is exceeded by a negative transaction utility. For example, we do without a soft drink during the match at the stadium or from the hotel room minibar because we consider the price exorbitant.

An amusing experience relating to overcharging occurred last summer at Porto Cervo, the famous tourist resort in Sardinia. I was taking a stroll with my family in the main shopping streets when at a certain point we decided to stop for a drink at an outdoor cafe. Arriving in the central square, we sat down on the terrace of one of the open bars, elegantly furnished with comfortable armchairs and wicker tables. The price list was very simple. Water, aperitifs, liquor, coffee, all had the same price of €25. Exchanging glances with my wife, my sister and my brother-in-law, I sat back and said: 'Guys, let me perform a little experiment. I'll pay €100 to buy us all a drink. But we have to stay here at least an hour. Trust me'.

What followed was one of the most entertaining spectacles in pricing psychology I have ever witnessed. In the space of an hour at least five couples had arrived, sat down, picked up the price list and then had got up and left while making sour comments or sarcastic remarks. Some tried their best not to be noticed by the waiters, others confronted them openly in a none too friendly manner. I was an outside observer, but judging by their clothes and jewellery, I concluded that this flight was not necessarily determined by limited financial means. The expression on their faces was in fact more disgusted than frustrated. It was not that they had just realized they were not wealthy enough for Porto Cervo, but rather that Porto Cervo demanded too much of their money.

Observing the waiters at my leisure, I realized that this high number of defections was fully incorporated into the timing of the service at the tables. A few minutes after we sat down – and after recovering from my initial shock at the prices – I had complained to my wife, saying that with these prices and with the fact that the place was empty, they could at least have deigned to serve us within a decent time. The long wait was far from being due to bad service however; on the contrary, the waiters were in fact giving customers plenty of time to see the price list, decide what to do and leave if desired. Approaching them immediately would have put many clients in the difficult position of having to having to say to the waiter's face that they were leaving, face paying a price they considered unacceptable or, worst of all, leave without paying the bill. The long wait was in fact a truly customer-oriented strategy and by no means a sign of bad service or ploy to keep the few customers seated at the tables so that the bar would not seem empty.

If it is thus true that the price influences the perceived utility of a product, in accordance with proximity to an expected reference price, it would be logical to expect that the measurement of transaction utility should in turn be determined by the difference between the price of the deal and the reference price. This means that the size of this difference will be perceived according to its proportional (i.e. not absolute) weight in relation to the original price.

In his classic work on pricing, Georg Stigler (1961) argues that, for a given level of acquisition utility and of spending power, a consumer will continue to seek additional price offers until the expected saving to be obtained equals the additional cost involved in finding the lower price. Let us take the example of a lady doing her weekly shopping at the street market. According to Stigler, she will continue moving from one stall to another looking for cheaper prices until she is convinced that further searching is pointless in terms of finding prices substantially lower than those already identified.

The importance of the price per se permits a more exact statement of this thesis, as follows: consumers will continue to seek additional price offers until the expected saving as a proportion of the total price is equal to the expected marginal cost of the search. The hedonistic principle underlying this phenomenon shows a strong parallelism with Weber–Fechner's law in psychophysics which states that the minimum change in a stimulus which is perceptible will be proportional to the stimulus. In our case, if the stimulus is the price, this law implies that the relationship between minimum difference in the price which is perceived and the average price is a constant. In other words, the lower the initial reference price, the smaller the variations in price which are perceptible.

Let us examine the case where discounts of the same size in absolute terms are applied to products having widely different reference prices. In an experiment conducted by Tversky and Kahneman (1981), a group of 93 people was asked to imagine a situation in which, as they are buying a jacket costing $125 and a calculator costing $15, the shop assistant informs them that the calculator is on sale in another branch of the store which is 20 minutes away on foot. In a second version of the experiment conducted with a group of 88 people, the question was modified with the prices of the products inverted, so that the calculator cost $125 and the jacket $15. The discount of $5 continued, however, to be applied to the calculator, which was thus on offer at $120. On being asked if they would be prepared to walk for 20 minutes in order to save $5, 68 per cent of the participants replied affirmatively in the first case, where the calculator cost $15, whereas only 29 per cent said they were willing to make this effort in the second case, where the calculator had a price of $125. Note that in both cases the total expenditure varied from $140 to $135 (Fig. 2.4).

This experiment proves that the value associated with saving a given amount depends on the starting price. Saving $5 seems very attractive if referred to the purchase of a calculator costing $15, but pretty low in the context of a starting price of $125 (and probably imperceptible in relation to the purchase of a $20,000 automobile). The value of a discount is perceived and measured therefore in percentage terms and not in absolute terms.

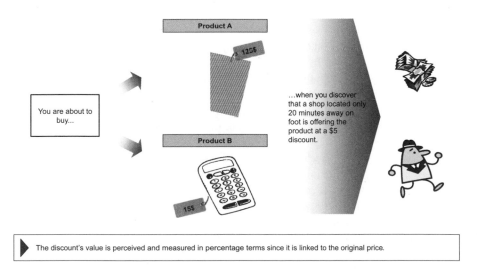

The discount's value is perceived and measured in percentage terms since it is linked to the original price.

Figure 2.4   The deal effect: what discount can influence my decision?

One of the basic flaws in the theory of the rational consumer demonstrated in the experiment is exactly this. The 20 minutes needed to reach the shop where the discount is on offer represent the cost of obtaining that discount. The rational question in this case is simply whether 20 minutes of my time is worth more or less than $5. If so, it is worth the effort of going to the other store and obtaining the discount. Otherwise, the effort makes no sense. The trade-off is clear: time in exchange for money or money in exchange for time. What counts is – according to the rational theory – the final state of my well-being, in this case as a specific combination of money and time.

However, consumer psychology does not work in this way. Once again, what counts is the initial reference context, the points of reference we use to assess a given transaction. In the case described, what the consumer takes into account is thus not the relationship between the saving in money terms and the cost in terms of time, but the relationship between the monetary saving and the reference price. It emerges clearly that saving $5 on a $15 purchase can be considered a real bargain, while saving the same sum on a $125 purchase is much less attractive. It is as if an inner voice tells us: 'Forget the $5. You can't miss out on a saving of 33 per cent, while one of 4 per cent is nothing special.'

A while ago I came across a similar case, with the difference that the good deal was not associated with the size of a discount but of a cost. I had just completed my check-out at the Sheraton hotel in Malpensa airport close to Milan when the desk clerk asked me if I wished to pay a €1 surcharge on the price of my room as a donation to Unicef. A small sum given in support of such a good cause undoubtedly represents – at least to my mind – a worthy contribution on the part of a person who is in a position to make it.

This request for a donation could have taken many other forms, which might have been equally manageable from an organizational point of view, such as a collection box strategically placed in the lobby of the hotel; alternatively, the question could have been asked at another moment when the client is at the desk, rather than at the precise moment when the bill is totted up and passed over for payment. From the point of view of effective communication, however, the mention of a €1 donation, directly after having named a figure running into a couple of hundred euros for a few hours' overnight stay in an up-to-date building in the middle of the Lombard countryside, had a certain efficacy. My first thought was in fact that it would be mean to refuse a small gesture in aid of the needy at the very moment when I was laying out a large sum of money in return for a single night of comfort. In that moment the price of the hotel room became my mental anchor, the reference point that I used in assessing whether or not to make the donation. Given the disproportion between what I was spending and the sum being asked in charity, donating €1 could only be viewed as an excellent deal. Further, and very intelligently, all I had to do was say 'Yes'. There was no need to scrabble in my pockets for coins or to change a note, just to sign my tab, which already listed the €1 of the donation. So, a good deal in every way, both affordable and simple.

2.3 POINTS OF REFERENCE

These factors naturally have fundamental implications for the structuring and presentation of pricing models as well as for managing the sales pitch when face to face with the customer. When for example the seller wishes to offer price reductions in return for desired patterns of purchasing behaviour or usage on the part of clients, it is essential to have a clear idea exactly which points of reference will be adopted by the client when assessing the various options being offered. The manner in which an identical situation can be perceived depends greatly therefore on the way it is graphically and conceptually presented, but in face-to-face communication with the client also on how the sales force manages the product presentation and the negotiation of the deal/price.

Let us examine a couple of interesting examples. Several banks have developed a special form of bank account with discounted fee structures which vary according to the assets invested by the client with the bank. In this kind of product the base fee for a premium account (i.e. a comprehensive account offering a large number of facilities) is pretty high, around €10 per month, but the discounts available are also substantial, in the region of €3 for every €100,000 invested. It depends on the presentation of the product whether the client receives it with greater or lesser enthusiasm and in fact it depends whether he interprets this as a 30 per cent discount on the normal monthly fee or whether he refers the figure to the context

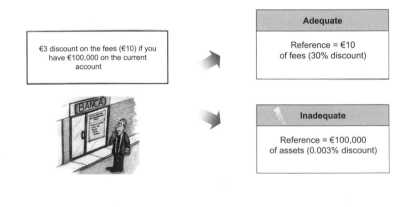

In terms of configuration and communication of pricing models and of sales pitch during the deal negotiation, it is important to guide the references clients will have when they evaluate the attractiveness of a given product.

Figure 2.5   The deal effect: which reference for a discount?

of the €100,000 invested. Bundling together the current account payment services and the deposit account investment services can then be perceived as a good deal as long as the reference point for the discount on services remains (Fig. 2.5).

IKEA in Italy offers an extremely enticing pricing model for its breakfasts which is also based on the concept of an excellent bundle deal. While the prices for the individual items are reasonable, but not exceptionally low (80 cents for a coffee or for a croissant, €1.20 for a cappuccino), the package price for coffee or cappuccino plus croissant is just €1. In comparison with the three possible individual purchasing intentions there is a substantial saving in percentage terms, and in one case in absolute terms. For the consumer intending initially to buy a coffee, the additional cost of the croissant is 20 cents compared to an original price of 80 cents, which represents a discount of 75 per cent. The same is true for the consumer intending only to eat a croissant who decides to take a coffee as well. An even greater discount can be obtained by taking a cappuccino with the croissant. Here the additional cost is 20 cents in relation to an original price of €1.20, thus yielding a discount of 83 per cent. But in the situation where one intended originally to have a cappuccino, the addition of a croissant will generate a negative additional cost, i.e. the customer will spend 20 cents less than he would have spent on the cappuccino alone.

It is interesting to note that the deal effect relating to this offer is further accentuated by the time limitation which is applied. These prices are available only until 10.30 p.m., i.e. at breakfast time. This 'happy hour' in reverse serves to further underline the good deal on offer.

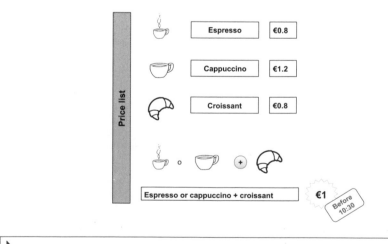

By offering a discounted menu for a set period of time (i.e. not a happy hour), IKEA clearly highlights the gain.

Figure 2.6   The deal effect: am I able to sell more products?

In his study on the pricing of *The Economist* magazine, Dan Ariely (2008) demonstrates the effective decision-making impact associated with an offer configuration clearly representing good value. The offer available via the Internet for the English weekly publication consisted of three options: a yearly Internet subscription priced at $59, a subscription to the printed version for $125 and – here is the point – a package including both the online and print subscriptions for $125. Basically, for customers who had initially intended to acquire the Internet version, to receive the print version as well would entail an additional cost of $66 (just over half the normal figure of $125). But an even better deal would be obtained by those who had initially intended to buy the print version, because in this case the additional cost of the Internet version would be $0, i.e. the best deal possible.

The 100 students participating in the study who were asked to choose one of the three options appeared to follow exactly this type of reasoning. Only 16 per cent of them opted for the Internet version and 84 per cent for the combined package, while nobody chose the print version alone. However, the idea that four-fifths of the students had a genuine preference for the Internet + print package seemed to be contradicted by the second part of the study, in which the choices were reduced to two, the Internet version alone or the Internet + print package, thus excluding the option of the print version alone. In this case, the students' choices showed a complete reversal, with 68 per cent opting for the Internet version and only 32 per cent for the package. Evidently the fact of having eliminated the print version alone had reduced the attractiveness of the package, causing a major shift to the Internet.

The wide divergence in the results of the two experiments – incidentally much bigger than that observed in my study relating to current accounts and credit cards – reinforces the main argument of this chapter, which is that there is no such thing as a stable preference. On the contrary, our choices are strongly influenced by the context, in particular by the manner in which this causes various options to appear as representing better or worse value. From the point of view of the theory of rational choice, the print alone option present in the first phase of the study was immaterial in that it was clearly sub-optimal compared to the package subscription available at the same price. The distribution of the preferences should therefore have been essentially the same in the second phase where precisely the print only option was lacking. This did not happen because the print only option included in the first phase took on the role of attractivity multiplier in relation to the combined package. When this was lacking, the distribution of the preferences was inverted. According to the classical theory of consumer choice, the alternative products do actually strongly influence the buying decision. However, they do so not only in the sense that they reduce the change of the original product to be sold, but sometimes also the other way around, i.e. by actually increasing this possibility.

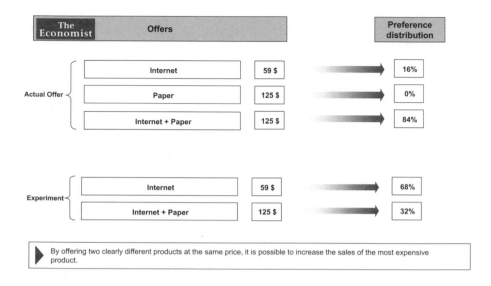

By offering two clearly different products at the same price, it is possible to increase the sales of the most expensive product.

Figure 2.7   The deal effect: an intelligent offer

2.4 PRICE AND QUALITY

A further interesting anomaly concerns the relationship between price and quality. In principle, this relationship should be simple: the better the quality of a product the higher the willingness to pay for it. Products of poor quality should be cheap, those of high quality expensive. In the end, quality has a cost and therefore it is right that this should be reflected in the asking price. Moreover, the quality of a product should increase its utility and hence the price we are willing to pay in order to obtain it. Of course, there are situations in which, over and above a certain level of quality, the marginal utility resulting for the consumer is minimal or even negative. Examples of this are those cases where the excessive number of features in a product makes it too difficult to use. Think of all the items of consumer electronics (TVs, telephones, cameras, video cameras, etc.) where we are able to master only a small proportion of the functions available; or, conversely, think of the success obtained by Apple with its strategy directed towards user-friendliness and minimalistic design.

Although it is generally true that high quality leads to and justifies a high price, sometimes, when the consumer possesses insufficient information concerning the true quality of a product, this relationship can be inverted. In these cases, the price becomes an indicator of the product's quality and, in a circular process, determines the associated willingness to spend. In order to establish this empirically, Ariely (2010) performed an interesting experiment in which participants were asked to evaluate the effectiveness of a painkiller offered at widely different prices. In the first phase of the study, electrodes were attached to participants' wrists and electric shocks were administered at varying levels of intensity ranging from barely perceptible to decidedly painful. After each shock, participants were invited to indicate the level of pain perceived, by using a mouse to click on a bar on the computer screen whose two ends were marked, respectively, 'not painful at all' and 'very painful'. At this point doses of painkiller were administered and participants were told that the full effect of these would be felt after 15 minutes. At the end of this time, the participants again received electric shocks of varying strength via the electrodes, after which they were invited to state whether the painkiller had been effective, i.e. whether the level of pain perceived had diminished or not. The interesting result that emerged from this was that all the participants who had received the painkiller priced at $2.50 per dose declared a reduction in the level of pain, while of those receiving the alternative priced at $0.10 per dose, only half had perceived a reduction in the level of pain. Of course, both products were identical and were not in fact painkillers, but simple capsules containing vitamin C, i.e. a placebo.

In another study along very similar lines conducted with a group of 29 students at the University of Iowa a very similar result emerged. The 13 students who had paid the full price for an anti-flu jab rated its efficacy in warding off winter ailments at a much higher level than the 16 students who had paid a discounted price.

These experiments demonstrate a very interesting characteristic of the quality/price relationship. This is that the price can influence the quality expected of the product and this in turn can influence the level of quality which is actually perceived. This means that paying a high price for a product can influence the perceived utility deriving from its use, which then acts to justify the high price paid. The price can therefore constitute an *indicator*, but also a *generator*, of quality. In this second case, the greater the sacrifice which must be made in order to own a product, the greater the utility of that product. The function determining the buying decision is transformed from:

$$(U - P) \text{ to } U(P) - P$$

where U stands for utility, P for price and P is a factor which can simultaneously increase or reduce U.

The price thus becomes an integral part of the product, no longer the counterpart in the sense of the sacrifice to be made for its ownership, but 'part and parcel', a constituent. It is the 'high' price itself that represents the bargain. The orientation 'high quality justifies high price' changes into 'high price generates high quality', unconsciously modifying our expectations and enhancing the experience of the product in our eyes, thus amounting to an excellent deal all round.

CHAPTER 3

THE SENSE OF POSSESSION

Economic theory states that at the end of the day, all direct costs (out-of-pocket costs) can be interpreted as opportunity costs. The former are the costs associated with doing a certain thing, the latter with *not* doing it. When for example we buy a shirt we will have an out-of-pocket cost corresponding to the price of the shirt and an opportunity cost equivalent to an article such as a polo shirt that we could have bought with that money instead of the shirt. This line of reasoning naturally presupposes a finite limit to our monetary resources at the time of the purchase (the so-called budget constraint) and in some cases also time limitations (in the sense of finding the time to make good use of the new item we have purchased). When we buy the shirt, for example, we will deploy monetary resources which will no longer be available for the purchase of the polo shirt. Moreover, at the time when we are using the shirt, we would not (normally) be able to simultaneously make use of the polo shirt.

When we assume that these two types of costs are the same it means that in effect we are postulating that all costs should be considered as opportunity costs, insofar as laying out money to acquire given goods or services automatically excludes alternative options of expenditure. The true cost of the shirt is therefore measured in terms of the other items we are obliged to forgo in order to purchase it.

3.1 OUT-OF-POCKET COSTS AND OPPORTUNITY COSTS

While attractive from a theoretical point of view, the identification of out-of-pocket costs with opportunity costs does not appear empirically valid. The value we assign to a product before we buy it tends to be lower than the value we ascribe to it once we have acquired it. In a purchasing situation, the out-of-pocket costs in cash terms which we need to sustain in order to buy a product appear to be seen as greater than the opportunity costs which we incur by not buying that product. In a selling situation, this mechanism is inverted. In this case, the out-of-pocket costs represented by the loss of the product being sold are perceived as greater than the opportunity costs associated with the money we forgo in order to keep it.

Basically, other factors being equal, it is the fact of being the seller or the buyer which makes the difference.

It is not true therefore that the consumer thinks always in terms of opportunity costs, or rather in terms of out-of-pocket costs being transformed into opportunity costs. Rather, he tends to think simply in terms of out-of-pocket costs, which in the moment of buying are represented by the money needed in order to gain ownership of the product, while in the moment of selling they are represented by the loss of the product itself. The related opportunity costs appear to play a lesser role. It is exactly this lack of symmetry which gives rise to the disparity between price or purchasing value on the one hand and price or selling value on the other hand. In essence, spending a sum of money in order to make a purchase seems to be less acceptable than not receiving the same sum through a sale.

When in 1979 Daniel Kahneman and Amos Tversky published the article which gave birth to behavioural economics and which led to Kahneman's being awarded the Nobel prize for economics in 2002, one of the key messages they sought to convey was related to precisely this asymmetry of value functions. People judge the value of an option in terms of an improvement or of a deterioration with regard to an existing state of affairs and not in relation to its influence on an overall end-state of well-being. The value we assign to an improvement is less, and opposite, to that we assign to a deterioration of equal dimension in absolute terms. Thus, contrary to the claims of rational consumer theory, these values are not considered as part of a global calculation which includes all other factors, but simply referred to the situation in which we find ourselves. If we go to the casino with €1,000 in our pocket and leave with €1,500 after winning €500 we will be much happier than when we go with €2,000 and leave with €1,500 after losing the same sum. The end result is the same – €1,500 – but the perceived value changes completely in the alternative scenarios. Furthermore, losing €500 is less acceptable than winning the same sum is welcome and so, if we went to the casino twice, first winning then losing an identical sum, we would be less happy than if we had not been at all.

The difference between the decision-making importance of out-of-pocket costs and of opportunity costs can thus be explained by reference to the asymmetry of the value function. While out-of-pocket costs represent a direct loss, opportunity costs are simply a missed chance. If, given similar objective values, losses are felt more than gains, then it is normal that out-of-pocket costs are felt more than opportunity costs.

In 1991 Kahneman, Knetsch and Thaler conducted an experiment designed specifically to establish this thesis, namely that a completely different value can be assigned to the same object according to whether it is already possessed, where losing it represents a loss (out-of-pocket cost), or whether it is available but not procured, with the forfeit of a possible gain (opportunity cost). In this experiment, a group of students was divided into two subgroups quite randomly. In one subgroup each person received the gift of a mug, while those in the other subgroup did not. At this point, the groups were invited to bargain freely for the sale or purchase of the mug. The aim was to establish, on the one hand, what price those in possession of the mug would charge to sell it, and on the other hand, what price those not in possession of a mug would be prepared to pay in order to acquire it. The experiment showed that the group possessing the mugs (the 'sellers') were willing to sell them for an average price of $5.25, while those without mugs (the 'buyers') were not prepared to pay more than an average of $2.75, thus confirming the hypothesis that the simple fact of owning an object tends to make the individual owning it value it more highly than he would if he did not possess it.

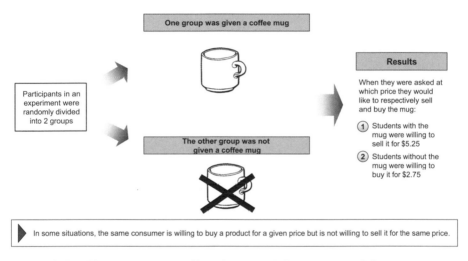

In some situations, the same consumer is willing to buy a product for a given price but is not willing to sell it for the same price.

Figure 3.1   The endowment effect: how much is a mug worth?

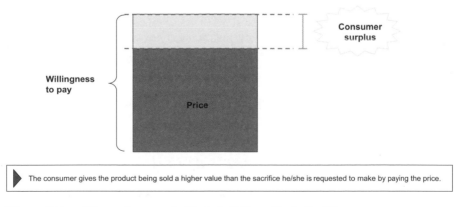

The consumer gives the product being sold a higher value than the sacrifice he/she is requested to make by paying the price.

Figure 3.2   The endowment effect: is it the seller's fault?

What is the origin of this gap? The concept of the consumer surplus is a possible starting point for explaining the phenomenon being examined. In this case the reluctance to sell or to buy the same item at a given price is explained by the fact that in reality the consumer assigns a higher value to a product than the price paid to purchase it. In the language of economics, the price does not correspond to the maximum buying price of the consumer. It follows logically that if the purchased item has a higher value than the price that was paid, the buyer will not be prepared to sell it for that same price.

The consumer surplus is thus defined as the difference between the value associated with a given item and the price paid to obtain it. Let us imagine that we have just bought an apartment for a particularly good price, for example because the former owner was obliged to sell quickly as a result of a gambling debt. In this situation we may assume that we would be very pleased with the deal we had just done and so would not be prepared now to sell the apartment for the same price. To persuade us to do so, a potential buyer would have to offer a higher price, sufficiently high to cover the consumer surplus obtained when we paid less for the house than the amount it was worth for us.

Determining the price which corresponds exactly to the maximum buying price is naturally not easy. In the experiment the researchers were apparently able to do this by setting up what we might term a 'recursive auction', in which the goods bought and sold were initially distributed at random, and by giving participants an incentive to offer or demand a good price, at the risk of losing out on a favourable transaction.

In the real world, however, companies tend to calculate their prices by reference to the 'cost-plus' model, thus limiting their ability to identify the maximum price obtainable. In this approach the first step is to establish the input cost of the product being priced, after which a mark-up is added corresponding to the profit the company intends to derive from the product in question. Quite apart from the difficulty of determining precisely the marginal costs (fixed and variable) effectively associated with the product, this method provides no way of fixing a price which reflects the consumer's maximum buying price.

In principle, the costs associated with a product's development, production and distribution should together make up the utility (and hence the willingness to buy) which will be generated by the product in the eyes of the consumer.

However, this correspondence is far from clear. Think for example of the phenomenon referred to as 'over-engineering', where extraneous functions are built into the product which are not used by the consumer, and which therefore do not generate utility. But think also of the various overheads in terms of organization and/or control which can have only an indirect impact on the attractiveness of the product. These are some of the reasons why cost-plus pricing cannot easily be used to determine the maximum buying price for a product.

With the use of this method it is thus possible that the difference between the maximum buying price and the minimum selling price is due not to the endowment effect, but simply to sub-optimal pricing of the product, in which its pricing (and hence profit) potential is not fully exploited.

Another classic method used by companies to determine prices is by reference to the competition. In this case the idea is for the seller to view himself as a 'price-taker', adapting his own pricing to that of the main competitors. There are two types of assumptions (not always explicit or conscious) underlying this approach.

The first is that competitors' prices are somehow correct in terms of consumer orientation. The second is that the consumer is aware of and genuinely compares the price with that of competitors, leaving very little room for manoeuvre or differentiation.

Neither of these assumptions is necessarily correct. On the contrary, experience shows that they are rarely so. A market based on competitor-oriented pricing is a market in which players are more focused on their competitors than on their customers. In this type of market, it is easy to find companies that know their competitors' prices, but difficult to find companies making systematic and expertly conducted studies of consumer preferences and maximum buying limits, and hence the elasticity of prices.

The question of a predisposition on the part of consumers to compare the prices of the various options available is in any case a very complex issue and relates to a far from universal practice. Naturally, there are a certain number of clients who pay particular attention to the price and whose buying decisions are strongly influenced, or even determined, by this factor. However, this relates to a relatively limited segment of the clientele and, even in these cases, not all of the prices available will be subjected to this comparison. At the supermarket for example, particular attention will be paid to the prices of staples such as pasta, but not necessarily to those of items such as the recharge for the air freshener. In the bank, the monthly fees payable will receive close scrutiny, while the cost of a bank transfer will not, and so on.

The absence of precise monitoring of consumer preferences thus leads, even in the context of competitor-oriented pricing strategies, to situations in which the market price does not reflect the maximum buying price the consumer is willing to pay. As in the case of 'cost-plus' pricing, the competitor-oriented approach can therefore lead to cases in which the difference between the maximum buying price and the minimum selling price is not in fact ascribable to the endowment effect, but simply to sub-optimal pricing levels.

A second possible explanation for this effect is based on the concept of transaction costs. The idea here is that taking possession of an item presupposes a process costly in itself, a process which can also be extended to the moment of sale, further increasing the costs. There must therefore exist a gap between the buying and the selling price sufficient to absorb the transaction costs and thus to generate a positive overall utility value. The selling (or transaction) costs are typically those associated with finding an interested buyer, ensuring that this buyer has both the means and the intention of paying the asking price and, lastly, those relating to the transportation and delivery of the item sold (Fig. 3.3).

We might for example no longer be interested in selling the apartment because we would not be able to recoup the conveyancing and banking charges we incurred in buying it, nor, possibly, the value of the time we spent in finding it and negotiating the deal. In this case we might be prepared to sell the apartment on only if the price offered included a margin sufficient to recover all these transaction costs, both material and immaterial.

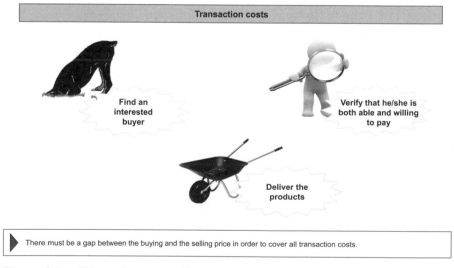

> There must be a gap between the buying and the selling price in order to cover all transaction costs.

Figure 3.3   The endowment effect … or transaction costs?

3.2 LOSSES AND GAINS

While these explanations clearly have a broad empirical application, they do not seem entirely to cover the divergence between purchasing and selling values which emerged from the study we examined above. In the experiment involving the mugs, the consumer surplus does not seem to have played a role, in view of the random separation of buyers and sellers and of the simple market clearing mechanism utilized to determine the transaction prices, together with the marked divergence between buying price and selling prices which emerged. Further, given the character of the experiment, no transaction risk or cost of any kind was imposed on participants by 'the market'.

The most reasonable explanation of the phenomenon thus consists in assuming the existence of an endowment effect, whereby the fact in itself of possessing an object increases its value, especially at the moment of determining whether to sell it.

As we have seen, the hedonistic principle underlying this mechanism derives from the fact that, other things being equal, losing something is less acceptable than failing to acquire it. A loss represents an out-of-pocket cost, while an unrealized gain corresponds to an opportunity cost. The former will be given greater weight than the latter, thus generating a mismatch, or disvalue, between the two types of costs (or prices) under consideration.

Following Thaler (1987), let us imagine a wine connoisseur who is willing neither to buy a particular bottle for $35, nor to sell it for $100 should it be already in his cellar. This represents a fairly 'classic' case study which is nevertheless paradoxical from the point of view of the theory of rational choice. The paradox rests on the gap between the maximum buying price, which here amounts to less than $35, and the minimum selling price, here amounting to $100 plus, in regard to the same object. The bottle of wine is worth less than $35 'in', but more than $100 'out', so to speak. Why? Once again, because of the endowment effect. Selling the bottle means suffering a loss with regard to something already possessed, whereas buying it equates to a gain. For the same object, in a buying situation the loss (of money) is seen as greater than the possible gain (of wine), while in the selling situation the loss (of the bottle) is viewed as greater than the possible gain (of money). The resulting maximum buying and minimum selling prices are different and depend on which role is envisaged in the transaction – that of seller or buyer.

This mechanism naturally also comes into play in regard to the sum of money involved in the transaction, depending whether the sum is paid or received. Money payable (i.e. already possessed and which must be forfeited) for the bottle can be viewed as a loss, while money to be received (i.e. not yet possessed but due) for the sale of the bottle can be interpreted as a gain. This attachment to money or even miserliness might be explained by the particular importance associated with its possession. The saying 'it's easy to be generous with other people's money' articulates the same idea seen from the opposite point of view: for other people's possessions, we tend to think it is easy to part with them (Fig. 3.4).

An interesting application of the endowment effect in a commercial context is the practice of offering a few weeks' trial period, during which the buyer has the right to return the goods without incurring any penalty. The sound technology manufacturer Bose, for example, advertises its Quiet-Comfort 15 headphones with a money-back guarantee if the customer is not fully satisfied. This is not the standard guarantee applying to a defective or malfunctioning product but a clear commitment to return the sum paid if the customer is in any way dissatisfied. One of the aims is obviously to build trust both in regard to the manufacturer and to the product. By promising to take the goods back in case of dissatisfaction, Bose is saying that it has nothing to hide and that it expects that the client's experience of using the product will be judged in a positive light. On the client's part, it means minimizing the risks associated with purchasing the product, because he has the faculty of changing his mind on the basis of the *experienced utility* obtained through sustained use in the real world rather than the *expected utility* deriving from reading the description or from a brief product test in the store.

As it happens, I myself have used the QuietComfort 15 headphones for over two years and I can vouch for their effectiveness. The last time they featured in a conversation was in response to a question from a fellow-passenger in the next seat

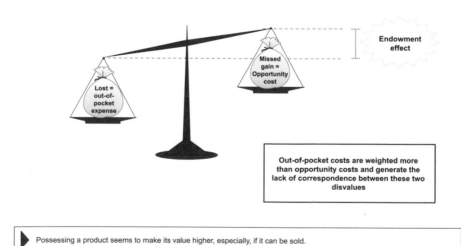

Possessing a product seems to make its value higher, especially, if it can be sold.

Figure 3.4   The endowment effect: can ownership of the product affect the choice?

on a flight from Munich to Madrid. Waiting until I had replaced them in their case in preparation for landing, he asked me if they really did reduce outside noise as claimed in the advertising. Having observed the smile that greeted my affirmative response, I believe I confirmed the old maxim that there's no better publicity than a satisfied client. However, customers will not always have an opportunity to discuss products they are buying with other clients – even if social networking technologies have dramatically extended the possibilities in this direction. For this reason, the offer of a trial period can be an excellent way to allow customers to experience the qualities of a product at first hand.

Another aim – or perhaps effect – of this type of guarantee is that of creating some kind of psychological 'lock-in' effect, by enabling the customer to view the product as his own, thus decreasing the chances that it will be returned, precisely because of the endowment effect. In principle, the fact of taking a product home for a trial period is no guarantee in itself of a genuine purchasing intention. If the transaction costs (e.g. the time and effort of taking the item home and then taking it back after a few weeks) are less than its expected utilization value over the period in question, the rational consumer will acquire the product even if he has no intention of keeping it right from the start. The wager taken by the seller is, however, that, even in such cases, the short period in question will suffice for the consumer to start perceiving it as his own, thus attributing to it a higher value than he would have done just a few days before.

Going back to our earlier analysis, the difficulty involved in returning a product we have taken home with us seems therefore to derive from the fact that this will be felt as a direct loss, hence an out-of-pocket cost, while not returning it will constitute no more than an opportunity cost, in the sense of forfeiting the reimbursement of the money originally spent. The greater detriment experienced in relation to an out-of-pocket cost in comparison with an opportunity cost will increase the value of the product and diminish that of the money reimbursed, thus making it more unlikely that the item will be returned.

Naturally, consciously opportunist behaviour on the part of the consumer does not represent the norm. Generally, when a client goes to the trouble of paying for a product, taking it home and, where relevant, installing it, the normal intention is to keep it. In such cases, the endowment effect will simply amount to a further subconscious lever encouraging the customer to retain the item over time, while the trust effect will serve to facilitate the initial sale by reducing the level of commitment involved. These two effects will therefore act together to render the 'buy it, try it, return it' sales formula even more attractive – and less risky – for products at a certain pricing level and for low-frequency or one-off purchases.

It is worth emphasizing that in mature markets, or ones that are highly regulated in terms of consumer protection such as are to be found in Western countries, companies need to master the use and coordination of these two effects. On one side, special offers, promotional activities and various other 'push' strategies used in marketing to induce consumers to make an initial purchase are becoming ever more aggressive and widespread. Take the increasing reliance on the concept of 'free', or the exponential growth of the business model exemplified by Groupon. On the other hand, new consumer legislation is increasingly directed towards the reduction of barriers to exit for consumers and towards offering them longer and longer time periods in which to change their mind or return goods.

These two tendencies will have the combined effect of rendering the consumer ever more volatile, creating further difficulties in promoting customer loyalty, and even in closing individual sales. Seeing a customer leaving the shop, the branch, or (in particular) the online store with a product will be increasingly less likely to guarantee a faithful long-term client. It will also be less likely to ensure that the product in question has been definitively sold and that it will not be returned in the ensuing weeks. Consumer 'cherry-picking' will increasingly be accompanied by 'cherry-backing'. The ability to capitalize on the endowment effect will indubitably be a key factor in countering this trend.

3.3 WHAT IS POSSESSED AND HOW

The question therefore is, what can companies do in order to accentuate this endowment effect? For sure, personalization of the product at the moment of purchase and its later configuration can be very effective means to this end. Almost all technology products, be they computers, smartphones, TV sets or videogames, now require an initial registration procedure together with the definition of a number of basic user parameters such as volume, ringtones, language, screen display, and so on. While this type of thing can appear banal or even irritating, the effect is generally to create some kind of personal connection with the object itself.

For example, when I switch on my iPhone, the first thing I see is a photo of my smiling wife, and with a few touches I can find the apps I use most frequently, handily placed for accessibility, while with a few more I can access the phone numbers and email addresses of my close contacts. It is true that all this wears off quite quickly. But it is also true that the absence of these personalized settings (and their convenience) is noticed very quickly when they are not present. When I try to make a call or listen to music with my wife's iPhone, I realize almost immediately that I'm dealing with an extraneous object, even if technically it is an identical telephone.

The Nintendo Wii console even attempts to make an amusement out of this process of configuration and personalization. For instance, the system enables you to give a name and an identity to the players through the selection of a number of options of facial features. This includes the colour and the cut of the hair, the shape of the eyes, etc. Within minutes, from being a soulless machine, the console is saving our scores under our own name, making us smile when we win, telling us off if we don't practise enough, and so on.

It seems incredible, but technical details such as this can really influence our human behaviour patterns and, more specifically, increase our sense of possession and hence our attachment to the device. The American psychologist B.J. Fogg (2003) invented the term 'captology' precisely to convey this idea. Of course, such mechanisms do not last indefinitely. On the contrary, they frequently lose their appeal very quickly. We are rapidly inured to them, and they can become tiresome and repetitive. The initial enthusiasm they provoke is, however, more than enough to ensure that the consumer develops that sense of possession which can increase a product's perceived value and thus reduce the risk of its being rapidly returned.

It is important to note that the sense of possession we have been discussing has in fact a dual connotation. The first corresponds to the generic attachment to one's own possessions which most of us feel with regard to various types of objects (and not only!). Often we start to feel affection for things because we associate them with fond memories, because they have become familiar, because we have become skilled at using them or simply because of the sacrifices we made in order to acquire them. In these cases, the value we attribute to the product is placed at a much higher level than the cost of a similar or an alternative product available on the market. How many cellars, basements, attics and store-rooms are filled with objects (toys, clothes, books, souvenirs, and so on) which we would not sell at any price and yet which we would not now dream of buying even for just a few euros or even cents. How many old telephones, computers, and also clothes and shoes are still around because we are 'comfy' with them or because they feel 'part of us'?

The second connotation of the term 'possession' relates to a purely transactional context and refers not to the fact of possessing, but simply to gaining ownership. To understand this distinction let us return to the experiment of the mugs. The truly interesting thing about this study, in my view, was that the students began to attribute a higher value to the mugs *immediately after* having received them. In the experiment the participants' willingness to spend was measured over 3–4 transaction cycles taking place within just a few hours. The students had no time to develop affection for the mugs, they made no sacrifice to obtain them and nor did they associate them with any fond memories or particular skills. Absolutely not. Just a few minutes' possession was enough to generate the asymmetry between the value perceived by the sellers, those who had received the mugs and had to decide whether to forfeit them in exchange for money, and the buyers, or those who had not received the mugs but who were offered the opportunity to buy them at a certain price.

Many product marketing strategies make intelligent use of a combination of these mechanisms in order to increase the product's attractiveness for the consumer. The uniqueness or handmade character of the product, limited editions and collector's items are classic methods for increasing the perceived value of a given product through the (anticipated) pleasure or prestige deriving from its possession rather than through any increase in its functional utility. The simple fact of possession in these cases is united, however, with some kind of narrative, or 'mythology' which characterizes the love of one's own things, typically via mechanisms of association or transposition of memories. In this context we can speak of the strategy of exploitation of 'vintage' or 'retro' styles commonly used today in many product sectors. Montblanc, for example, makes use of this principle with its range of pens inspired by leading actresses of the American cinema in the '50s and '60s. Here, companies seek to reference the possibility, for owners of these products, of reliving the 'flair', or 'zeitgeist', the culture, thought-patterns and memories of a bygone era.

In some sectors the endowment effect is also going through a profound transformation with the digitalization of media content which can be distributed via the Internet at a minimal marginal cost. In regard to film, the 'rental' business model has coexisted with the 'purchase' model quite happily for 20 years, probably thanks to the mechanism we have been describing. Despite the widespread availability of films for rental at prices four or five times lower than the cost of purchasing, a certain segment of consumers has continued to buy movies to keep in their home collections. Obviously, in cases where the decision to purchase was based on the expectation of viewing the film a number of times, and thus amortizing the higher initial cost, this would be economically rational. However, it seems that more frequently other reasons motivated the consumer to buy the film. The convenience of obtaining the film, taking it home and viewing it with no further complications might certainly be seen as an advantage over the renting option, where it would be necessary to take the film back. But also, the satisfaction of having the film at home, of possessing it, of adding to one's collection, must surely be at least equally important. If I examine my collection of videocassettes, Blue Ray disks and DVDs I realize that in very few cases have I watched them more than once and almost never a sufficient number of times to justify, in economic terms, the difference between the buying price and the rental price. The attractiveness of the 'buy' business model emerges precisely from a combination of laziness and the endowment effect, even if it is obviously very difficult to disentangle the relative importance of each in any general way.

The growth of the video on demand model, as well as that of stores renting DVD or Blue Ray products which are delivered and returned by post, has upset this equilibrium. Sales of movies on DVD have been declining for years in the United States (the Blue Ray format has seen growth, but not sufficient to compensate these losses), while online distribution continues to grow. The war between telecoms companies, cable TV channels and online content providers is now focused on direct distribution. Even the big movie studios, suffering greatly from the decline in sales through traditional channels, are pondering over ways to reach their customers directly or at least to update their distribution models through collaborative ventures.

It is interesting to note that, in the long-standing contest between purchase and rental we have already described, the economic advantage of rental was balanced by the convenience of purchase. In today's new market, however, all the advantages lie with rental because downloading a movie is not only cheaper than buying it from a video store or supermarket (and indeed is completely free if downloaded from a pirate website!), but also much easier. It is no longer necessary even to leave the house either to get or to return a film. Just a few touches on the TV remote control or the computer mouse are sufficient to download, pay for and view the movie. This will make it increasingly difficult for the studios to exploit the endowment effect to push consumers toward the purchase rather than rental of films.

Nevertheless, some attempts are being made, notably through the idea of building up a personal video library or collection in the 'cloud'. The problem here will be that human beings, accustomed since the dawn of time to the physical ownership of possessions, have had only a short time in which to develop similar sentiments towards digital phenomena. Important writers – thinking for example of Jeremy Rifkin and his book *The Age of Access* – apparently put their money on exactly the opposite tendency, namely that the concept of ownership will increasingly give way to usage. I personally am not entirely convinced by this argument. Mankind is a creature of habit, but who is learning and evolving very rapidly. The physical nature of ownership will surely change, but not the sentiment in itself.

3.4 GIVING AND TAKING AWAY

Some reflection on the question of possession is important in relation to strategies for the development, publicizing and commercialization of a product. It will further have a bearing on sales strategies. There are many situations where the consumer has an option of purchasing a number of different versions of the same product ranging from a basic model to versions with additional features and/or accessories. In buying a new tablet, for example, a consumer can choose between an Internet-enabled version or a simple stand-alone version, or can opt for basic or extended memory configurations. Similarly, in choosing a new air-conditioner the choice is between an automatic or manual thermostat. It is often difficult for the consumer to know his precise needs in advance – whether the basic model is enough, or whether a mid-range or a premium version equipped with a multitude of features will be most appropriate.

In this type of sales situation – where the consumer is not able to define in detail which is the most appropriate configuration of price and product – there is scope to guide him towards versions of the product offering higher added value for him, which can correspond to a greater profit margin for the manufacturer. The endowment effect can play a key role in this. The idea is to present the product initially in a higher-end configuration, ensuring that the customer takes possession of it (even if only notionally), and then play on the product vs price trade-off emphasizing the value factor and minimizing the discount factor. Let us examine a concrete example.

Some years ago, following the birth of my first daughter, I decided together with my wife to change cars and to purchase a family model. To be frank, the initial screening was performed on the basis of two very simple criteria: the car had to be spacious and also well-designed. Our previous car had in fact been a two-seater convertible model that we were crazy about but which was absolutely unsuited to our new family situation. Taking leave of it was already difficult enough, so we wanted at least to move on to something which was not purely functional but which was also a little bit stylish. We opted for a 'comby' model produced by a German manufacturer. Fairly confident in our decision we paid a visit to the dealer in order to view it close-up and to get a better idea of the car itself as well as of the price.

After a few minutes we were approached by a salesman – let us call him Mr Black – who proceeded to embark on a very patient explanation of all the technical and functional features of the car (neither my wife nor I being exactly what you might call an expert, it was a far from simple job to get the message across). Having established a real interest on our part, Mr Black invited us to his desk, offered us a coffee and, continuing in his patient Socratic manner, began to draw up the car of our dreams. 'You want metallic trim, automatic gearshift, alloy wheels, this engine size … etc.' After 20 minutes or so, having completed the specification of all the special characteristics of the additional options included, he printed out three A4 sheets bearing the detailed description of the vehicle, feature by feature and accessory by accessory, and handed them to us. 'Here you are, Mr and Mrs Trevisan – this is the car that in my view you should buy. It has everything you need and it's a great automobile. Let's take a look together.'

Here he began, very calmly, to explain what he had included in the offer point by point and why each was important for us. 'The rear parking system is standard, but I have added it at the front because the car is pretty long and that can make it difficult to judge the distance', or 'With Bluetooth there's no need for leads, connectors and so on, you just program the system at the start and every time you get into the car, your mobile will be automatically connected to the speakers. It's simpler, but above all it's safer.' At the end of this process he concluded by adding: 'With this configuration the car has a price of X euros. With our excellent-value leasing program I can let you have it for a monthly payment of Y euros. The contract has a duration of three years and is inclusive of 20,000 km per year, with a down-payment of Z euros.'

At this point, at my somewhat shocked reaction to the level both of the overall price and of the monthly payments, together with my immediate request for a discount, Mr Black remained unruffled and once again detailed the exceptional value represented by the relevant configuration of the car. He did this, however, in a very astute manner, making use (possibly unawares) of the endowment effect. He said: 'Mr Trevisan, I realize that it is a lot of money. Unfortunately there is very little room for discounts on this type of model and we are doing everything we can to give you very favourable payment terms in comparison with going market rates. Certainly, I can reduce the price, but it will mean reviewing the configuration of the car. Take the European satellite navigation system. This has a list price of X euros, which corresponds to Y euros of the monthly payment. But is it really indispensable?'. My response was: 'Well, in fact I travel a lot between Italy, Austria and Germany. At the moment my navigator requires me to change DVD every time I cross the border and replace it with one that covers the country I'm entering. It's a real pain. Not having to do this would be far easier, I reckon I'll keep the European navigator'.

Mr Black's answer was: 'You're right. It can be a real nuisance. In that case, how about the leather upholstery? Price-wise and in terms of the monthly payments, it has a similar impact to the navigator. Maybe it's not really necessary.' My wife: 'I don't agree. Our daughter needs to play, she'll have dirty hands, she drops things, she might even feel unwell and … you know how kids are. Normal seat covers means desperately trying to clean them or having stained seats for the next three years.' 'Well, yes – replied Mr Black – I hadn't thought about that. But maybe we could do without the automatic gearshift. It'll save even more than the leather upholstery.' But my reply was: 'No way. The smooth gearshift was the thing I liked best about the car in terms of driving experience. Besides, my wife is not mad about driving in any case. If we take away the automatic shift she might not use the car at all.'

So, after an animated half-hour discussion, the car basically stayed configured in accordance with Mr Black's original specification. My request for a discount had been fended off by means of value arguments in which, in fact, I was constantly reminded of my desire for the new car, thus bolstering my willingness to spend. The conducting of the negotiation was a superb example of what is classically referred to as 'value selling', where the perception of value derived not only from the rational evaluation of a number of accessories, but also from the endowment effect originating from the initial configuration of the vehicle, the handing over of the cost breakdown, together with the salesman's calm and patient manner.

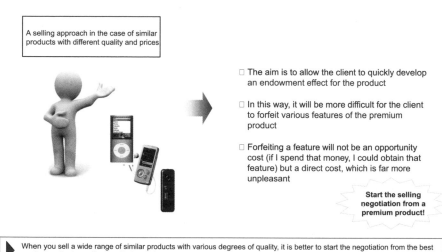

A selling approach in the case of similar products with different quality and prices

☐ The aim is to allow the client to quickly develop an endowment effect for the product

☐ In this way, it will be more difficult for the client to forfeit various features of the premium product

☐ Forfeiting a feature will not be an opportunity cost (if I spend that money, I could obtain that feature) but a direct cost, which is far more unpleasant

Start the selling negotiation from a premium product!

When you sell a wide range of similar products with various degrees of quality, it is better to start the negotiation from the best product and not specifically talk about prices.

Figure 3.5   The endowment effect: and in the case of similar products?

This example thus embodies an interesting strategy in regard to situations in which a range of similar options is available on a scale of increasing quality, or identical products having a number of varying configurations in terms of different features and accessories. In these cases it is advisable to begin by showing the client the top-of-the-range product, avoiding where possible any mention of price (and the resulting danger of exceeding the maximum buying price which the client may have determined), with the aim of encouraging the customer to acquire a feeling of possession in regard to the product in question. After this it will be difficult for the consumer to sacrifice any of the features and refinements of the premium product, precisely because this will no longer represent a variety of opportunity cost (if I spend this money I can obtain these additional features) but rather an out-of-pocket cost, which is much less acceptable (I can save money if I do without these features).

CHAPTER 4

AN EMBARRASSMENT OF RICHES

The efficient management of resources is one of the principal tasks of economic theory. One of the foundations of economics is to seek the greatest possible output with the minimum input. The limits on resources thus constitute a problem which must be faced. Conversely, an abundance of resources is an opportunity to be exploited. This also holds good in relation to different choices and buying options. Starting from the assumption that consumers are capable of evaluating the characteristics of the products and services available on the market, the greater the number of options available, the greater the chance that the most suitable offer will be found. A multiplicity of options thus signifies an increase in the expected utility of choice.

4.1 THE PROBLEM OF CHOICE

There are times, however, when the multiplicity of options represents a problem for the consumer and not an opportunity. A first example is when the choice in question has important psychological ramifications, i.e. in situations where the wrong decision can have strongly negative emotional repercussions. Not having to choose at that point takes on a positive connotation. By not choosing, the consumer may indeed have to face the negative consequences of a mistaken course of action or turn of events, but at least can avoid the weight of responsibility for a wrong choice (Fig. 4.1).

One market which seems to have adapted to consumers' preference for avoiding decisions is that for healthcare, specifically for the first dollar non-deductible type of healthcare insurance plan (Thaler 1980). At first sight, this type of option might not seem entirely rational from the insurer's point of view because it leads to a situation in which there is no marginal cost associated with making use of healthcare services, thus incentivizing their use. However, the value-function associated with this model corresponds precisely to the fact that many consumers are extremely uncomfortable with taking decisions which involve a trade-off between money and health, especially on behalf of third parties, such as children or the elderly. This reluctance will apply whichever way the decision

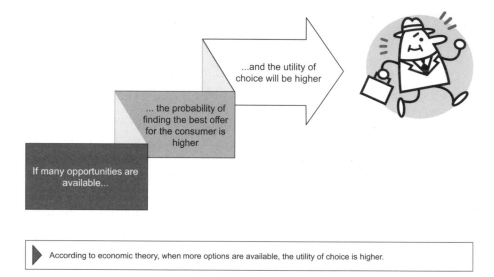

If many opportunities are available...

... the probability of finding the best offer for the consumer is higher

...and the utility of choice will be higher

▶ According to economic theory, when more options are available, the utility of choice is higher.

Figure 4.1   The paradox of choice: how does a rational consumer react?

goes. Let us take the case of a decision regarding whether or not to have a very costly diagnostic test. If we decide not to undertake the test, only for the disease to be discovered later, possibly at an advanced stage making treatment difficult, the sense of responsibility will be immense. On the other hand, if we have the test and nothing emerges, we may regret having incurred an unnecessary expense. Hence it is better to avoid making the decision by taking out an insurance policy which will cover the cost, thus avoiding the need for a trade-off between the known cost of the test and the unlikely contingency of having the disease.

The impact of the zero-deductible element in healthcare schemes was demonstrated empirically in Germany with the introduction of the 'Praxisgebühr', imposing a tariff of €10 on the occasion of the first medical visit in any three-month period. Almost immediately the number of visits fell dramatically, showing that the tariff had imposed a monetary cost on access to healthcare services which many patients were not prepared to pay. The decision to go to the doctor had suddenly acquired a financial aspect and the €10 charge had clearly introduced a disincentive to do so. As a result potential patients now faced a dual sense of responsibility.

This €10 obliged the patient to reflect more carefully on the need or otherwise to visit the doctor, obviously leaving him free to do so in cases of real need, but at the same time leaving him with the responsibility and the risk if he decides not to go. Where previously it had cost nothing to go, the new system introduced a trade-off between a known cost and an unknown risk. By thus redefining the terms of the pay-off, the fee makes the decision much more difficult.

When a few years ago I decided to change my medical insurer and my type of health insurance I too found myself faced with the decision of whether or not to choose a zero-deductible type plan. Mindful of its extraordinary impact on patterns of healthcare usage – and aware also of my likely reactions when faced with certain forms of incentive – I opted for the zero-deductible formula. Although this would involve much higher monthly payments, I did not wish decisions concerning the health of my family and myself to be influenced in any way by economic considerations. It is interesting to note that at the time of making this decision, I chose a further option allowing for the reimbursement at the end of the year of a proportion of the premiums paid if no claims were made during the period. Why did I accept this incentive 'after the event' to reduce my medical expenditure but not the incentive 'before the event'? I believe there were two reasons.

The first is that the costs associated with the non-zero-deductible type of policy represent immediate ('out-of-pocket') costs, requiring one to put one's hands in one's pocket up-front, while losing the end-of-year bonus represents an opportunity cost. As we saw in the last chapter, these, even if they are identical from a strictly economic point of view, are quite different in psychological terms. It is one thing not to recoup money already spent, quite another to have to face an additional expense – that is to say over and above sums already paid in premiums.

The second reason which induced me to opt for the 'after-the-event' reimbursement model was the different timing of the pay-off. The incentive not to go to the doctor in cases where one is not covered by a zero-deductible scheme is immediate, in that the money must be paid directly. Contrariwise, the reimbursement is shifted forward in time, in the sense that this money will be paid only at year-end. This time-lapse will often play a decisive role in our decisions, for the simple reason that an immediate sacrifice is far more vivid to our minds than the loss of a possible reward in the future. Taking this phenomenon into account I concluded that the prospect of receiving a refund on my premiums in the future would not, in all probability, strongly influence my decisions regarding medical visits, while knowing that I would be required to pay directly for treatment, up to a certain minimum threshold of expenditure (i.e. the non-zero-deductible system) might well do so (Fig. 4.2).

There is a second case where the abundance of choices can be negative for the consumer. Here it is the very multiplicity itself which causes the problem. In these cases the consumer has the cognitive problem, as it were 'before the event', of having to compare a large number of alternative products in order to determine which of them is most suited to his needs, together with the regret, 'after the event', at having been obliged to relinquish a number of interesting alternatives. Choosing thus becomes a mental strain in view of the mass of information to be processed before taking the decision, and a frustration in light of the many other opportunities missed after the decision.

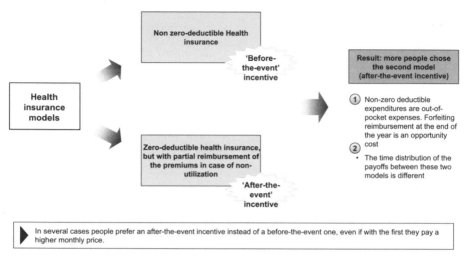

In several cases people prefer an after-the-event incentive instead of a before-the-event one, even if with the first they pay a higher monthly price.

Figure 4.2   The paradox of choice: incentive before or after the event?

As observed by Schwarz (2004), the number of products available in the majority of today's market sectors is absolutely huge and has increased exponentially in recent years. For the Italian market, we can cite for example the 126 types of pasta available at Esselunga supermarkets, 590,146 books at the Feltrinelli megastore, 333 colour TVs at Euronics, 140 channels available on Sky, 3,500 investment funds with Fineco. When the choices available reach this level, the tasks of gathering, evaluating and processing the information become enormous, requiring ever-increasing expenditure of time and energy. Social psychologists speak of doubts, anxieties and even fears associated with the need to choose.

This problem of the excessive number of options available does not relate only to direct choices, however. There are more and more contexts where, before we even begin the selection of the product or service that interests us, we must first decide on the channel and the means for making our choice. The world of e-commerce in particular offers us a plethora of sites and portals dedicated to the comparison of prices, special offers, specialist blogs, services offering information and special deals in relation to third-party producers, and so on. If for example we decide to invest money in shares or bonds, we need first to know which sources to refer to in order to get advice on the type of investment best corresponding to our profile, or which portal could allow us to locate and compare the most suitable options. Having done this we must then choose a specific product to be acquired as well as the best supplier in this regard. Lastly we have to decide where to take our money in order to complete the transaction. At each step we find a variety of market operators offering varying ranges of options, organized according to criteria and parameters which are not fully comparable, and each with a 'value chain' which is more or less applicable according to the precise circumstances. It may seem paradoxical, but investing €10,000 is more complex and more demanding today than in the past, despite the multitude of products, sources of information and distribution channels which are available (Fig. 4.3).

Lastly, the scope of our decisions has become enormously more extended. To remain in the world of finance, think of the varying requirements in connection with private pension plans, the investment of severance pay or bonuses, and with health insurance. In other spheres, the securalization and liberalization of our societies have brought much greater freedom of choice to aspects of life that, only 50 years ago, were far more rigidly determined. This includes the various forms of religious or spiritual activity, the growing number of date-matching services available which increasingly have come to resemble the personalized configuration of a product, the growing desire (or need) to pursue one's career abroad, the multitude of medical or cosmetic therapies available, and so on. In essence, there are more and more decisions to be taken, each involving a greater number of possible options than in the past (Fig. 4.4).

This leads to a dual problem. Each individual choice becomes more complex due to the large number of options available. But choice in general also becomes progressively more time-consuming because of the larger number of areas where it is required. For instance, we can dedicate ample time to our investment decisions, but this time will no longer be available for identifying and choosing the right job (another fundamental decision in our lives), for deciding on our healthcare insurance arrangements (which will ensure our well-being over time), for buying

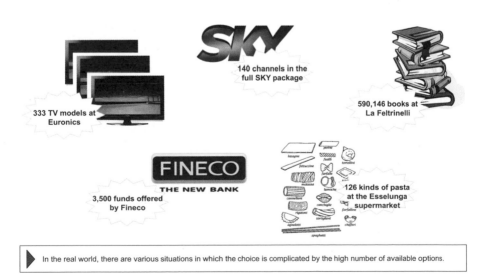

333 TV models at Euronics

140 channels in the full SKY package

590,146 books at La Feltrinelli

3,500 funds offered by Fineco

126 kinds of pasta at the Esselunga supermarket

In the real world, there are various situations in which the choice is complicated by the high number of available options.

Figure 4.3   The paradox of choice: and now? Which one?

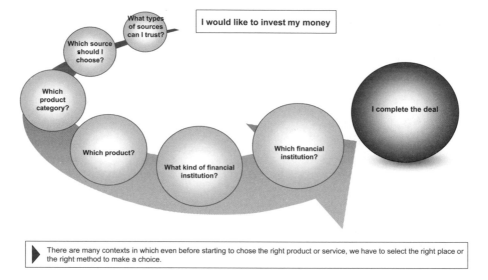

> There are many contexts in which even before starting to chose the right product or service, we have to select the right place or the right method to make a choice.

Figure 4.4   The paradox of choice: and if the choice is not limited to the product?

the right car (surely an important question, at least from the financial point of view) or TV, for watching an amusing movie, reading an intelligent book, finding a good restaurant, and so on. It is thus increasingly difficult for individuals to manage all these single decisions in a satisfactory manner. The accumulation factor in regard to this great number of (complex, even if not equally important) decisions we are required to face entails a further problem, which is the need to establish a relative order of priority for our choices and how much time and energy we should devote to each.

4.2 LESS IS BETTER THAN MORE

The fundamental question is therefore, how good are we at choosing in contexts where we are offered a multitude of options? In a study titled 'When choice is demotivating', Iyengar and Lepper (2000) placed a jam-tasting stand in a delicatessen where customers could sample the various flavours and receive a $1 discount voucher to be deducted from the normal price of a pot. In one version of the experiment, 24 different varieties of jam were available both for tasting and for purchase. In a second version, the flavours available for tasting were reduced to 6, while the full range continued to be available for purchase. The study showed that the success of the tasting stand, its effectiveness in attracting potential customers, was directly proportional to the number of different types of jam displayed, so that the stand with 24 varieties attracted more attention than the stand with only 6. While this did not seem to have any particular effect on the tasting itself, because the number of jams tasted remained the same, it did generate a substantial difference in buying decisions, because 30 per cent of participants in the experiment with only six types of jam on display actually went on to buy a pot, while only 3 per cent of potential consumers in the other group did so (Fig 4.5).

In a comparable study, one group of students was given the opportunity to try different types of chocolates and then were asked to rate them in terms of their pleasant taste. After this, in another room, they were offered a small box of chocolates in return for their participation in the trial. As an alternative they were offered the choice of cash. As in the previous example, one group had been offered 6 different types of chocolates for tasting, while for a second group the choice had been extended to 30 different types. As in the case of the jams, the students who had had a limited selection of chocolates were more appreciative of their taste and tended to choose the box of chocolates as a reward, with an incidence four times greater than the choice of cash.

Based on such fascinating empirical findings, large retailers are now seeking ways of reducing the number of products on display per square meter of shelves, precisely in order to prevent this excess of choice from leading to lower sales. Traditionally, stores have organized their range and stock of products on the basis of logistical, administrative and warehousing costs. In commercial terms, however, their rationale has always been to try to offer as many products as possible, convinced that by doing so they would be able to satisfy the broadest possible range of customer preferences. Evidence suggesting that, in any case,

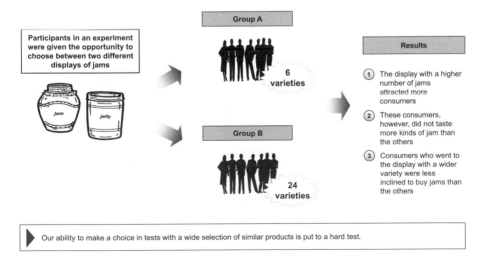

Our ability to make a choice in tests with a wide selection of similar products is put to a hard test.

Figure 4.5   The paradox of choice: am I a good decision-maker?

three-quarters of the alternative products to those habitually bought by a given customer are not even noticed by that customer, makes it necessary to find an optimal balance between the range of products and the attention generated. The idea that a large number of options is not always the best solution to this problem thus acquires added importance.

Even if no definitive conclusions are yet forthcoming in regard to this dilemma, a good hypothesis could be that a large number of options can be positive in terms of satisfying preferences in cases involving strong brands which are well-known. In situations, however, where familiarity with the products on display is low, an excess of options can in fact lead to a reduction in sales. This idea is based on the theory that in cases involving strong brands, the problems of product identification and selection are somehow already resolved in advance. Here, the visit to the supermarket no longer corresponds to the moment of choice in the classical sense, but simply to the physical acquisition of the product whose purchase has already been decided on beforehand.

Having settled the problem of the multiplicity of options and the possible confusion which can result, the only mechanism which continues to apply is the effective matching of the maximum possible number of consumer preferences with the availability of the corresponding products on the shelves. If consumers have a clear idea of what they are looking for, the availability of a large number of different products will obviously increase the probability of their finding what they seek. On the other hand, where the recognition, consideration and assessment of goods takes place at the point of sale, the availability of a large number of options can have the opposite effect, making the act of choice more difficult and even inhibiting it.

The hedonistic principle underlying this difficulty of selection corresponds to what we might call the paradox of opportunity costs. The greater the number of options available, the higher the probability that we will find the most pleasing one, which in turn will generate higher value. But at the same time, the greater the number of options, the greater the number of possibilities we must discard in order focus on the preferred one. The greater the number of different choices, the more that will necessarily not be explored. In reaching a final choice, we must simultaneously abandon a vast number of alternatives that we reject. And since in general losses are felt more strongly than gains of the same dimension, the expected utility deriving from the discarded options would appear greater than the experienced utility associated with the option chosen.

So for example the fact of choosing a thriller movie rather than a comedy can lead to a negative overall utility even if we preferred the first film, in itself, to the second. Seeing a film actually means missing out on another, which promptly acquires a higher value than it would have intrinsically if we saw it. In real life, however, for every film we see we miss out not on one, but on dozens of others. And this makes the situation even more complicated. When I installed a home video-on-demand system, for example, my first thought was: 'That's the end of sitting in front of boring TV shows. From now on, we can choose and watch any film we like, whenever we want.' The reality soon turned out a bit differently. My wife and I can easily spend 20 or 30 minutes deciding on a movie. This process is somewhat harrowing because we have no clear or rational method for determining our preference, each time instead going through a somewhat muddled process. This can include watching the various trailers, if available, reading the plot summary, referring to the cast, the director, or even the author. The result can be that we are more confused than we were to start with. In the end, after a sort of aimless tussling, we decide on a film (or not, because often we give up the task and watch what's available on the normal channels!). We pay and we start watching, with at least the first half-hour spent wondering why we chose this particular one (which we now view critically and with a certain detachment) and what the alternatives would have been like (much better, we imagine). This means that the need to weigh up how alternatives influence the way we perceive the choice (before the event) but also how we then judge the outcome (after the event). We suffer more in making a decision and we enjoy the result less.

This situation is further complicated by the multidimensional nature of the options in consideration. Standard economic theory maintains that the only opportunity costs we need to consider are those relating to the second-best alternative. In considering the alternatives to the movie we chose, we should not therefore worry about the entire movie collection available on our home video-on-demand service, but only about the film we would have chosen had the original one not been available. Even if it is very clear from the theoretical point of view, in practice this approach is problematic for the simple reason that the alternatives will possess multiple characteristics and may excel in any of them. The thriller may for example be outstanding in general, or in terms of suspense, but may not match the fun value of the comedy, the historical film's content, the dialogs of the drama or the science fiction movie's cinematography. When we watch the chosen film we therefore run the risk of finding the dialogs lacking in interest because we are comparing them with them with the excellence of those of the drama, the cinematography poor in quality in comparison with what we could have enjoyed in the science fiction film, and so on. It is almost as if we constructed an imaginary film in our minds which combines all these qualities of excellence and in comparison with which the actual film watched loses its appeal.

The result of being thus obliged to compare complex alternatives and to make a trade-off between the varying characteristics on offer is not only that of making the moment of decision more complex mentally and more stressful emotionally. In many cases it can even prevent people from deciding, by putting off the decision or simply by avoiding it. In an experiment performed by Tversky and Shafir

(1992), participants were described a situation where a shop was offering a Sony CD player for a very favourable price of $99 and were asked to say if they would decide to buy it or whether they would keep looking for an alternative model or brand. A second scenario was then described in which, as well as the Sony offer, the shop was also offering a luxury Aiwa model for $169, also heavily discounted. In the first case 66 per cent of the participants said they would buy the Sony product, while 34 per cent said they would wait. In the second scenario, 27 per cent of respondents said they would buy the Sony and 27 per cent the Aiwa, while 46 per cent said they would wait.

In a similar study, participants were offered $1.50 to fill in some questionnaires. After doing this, they were offered an alternative remuneration of a quality pen and were told that the pen had a normal price of $2. In a second version of the study the participants were again offered $1.50 in cash or the pen worth $2, but this time with a further option of two pens of lower quality but with a combined value of $2. Where in the first scenario 75 per cent of the participants had chosen the pen, in the second case only a combined total of 50 per cent opted for either the nice pen or the two lower-quality pens.

These examples show that the fact of adding a second option, transforming a simple decision which involves the assessment of a special offer on a single product into a comparison between two products, on both of which an attractive discount is offered, creates an inner conflict and strongly inhibits the ability to choose. Obliging the consumer to perform a calculation involving a trade-off between price and quality on more than one product may thus induce him or her to avoid or at least put off the decision. In discounting a number of products the risk is therefore that of obtaining a reduction in demand in place of the intended increase.

Conversely, the presence of a clearly favourable alternative, obviating the need to make a trade-off by weighing up the advantages and disadvantages of various products, can render the decision easier and clearer, in the sense of better-defined and immediate. In a third scenario for analysis in relation to CD players, Tversky and Shafir asked participants to imagine a situation where, together with the Sony discounted to $99, the shop offered a lower-quality no-name model at the normal price of $105.

Apart from a few participants who were evidently loyal to the Aiwa brand, the vast majority opted for the Sony inasmuch as it represented better value both in terms of quality and of price. The interesting point is that here 76 per cent of respondents indicated their intention to buy the Sony player, 10 percentage points more than in the original scenario where it had been the only product offered.

In other cases various alternatives may be assessed differently according to the need to accept or refuse each specific option. This is because, within a complex choice situation, what really counts is not the considered assessment of the overall characteristics of the various options, but the prominence or emergence of certain characteristics over others. Where overall values are equal, often those options offering more markedly positive single characteristics will tend to prevail in situations requiring the positive identification of the best alternative. These same options may however be discarded in cases where it is necessary to eliminate the worst alternative. Here it will be the prominence of the worst characteristics which determines the decision. The types of decisions that are taken thus depend on the context in which the decider evaluates the options. In this sense, when taking decisions of a multidimensional nature, people do not make some kind of mental algebraic calculation of the relevant plus and minus factors. What they do rather is to overvalue certain characteristics and undervalue others according to the circumstances, to the objectives and to their mental representations of the choices available, in a manner which will have a decisive bearing on the result of the decision-making process.

4.3 CHOOSING LESS, GETTING MORE

Such phenomena obviously have repercussions as far as sales strategies are concerned. In enumerating the selling points of a product it may be more productive to focus on fewer value functions (for example the high quality or the low price), in order to maintain simplicity by allowing the consumer to concentrate his attention on a small number of salient, and convincing, characteristics. When a single option is simultaneously characterized by both prominently negative and prominently positive qualities it is therefore important to decide for example whether it would be better for us to speak in positive terms of our product or in negative terms of the competition's. When the complexity of the choice combines with the need to weigh up the options in terms of a trade-off and provokes levels of difficulty, stress or anxiety which could inhibit or put off the choice of purchase, the role of the salesman in spurring or encouraging the client towards taking a decision becomes critical.

Technology can also be very helpful. Amazon for example has developed a highly sophisticated system to manage the immense range of its products. In the area of books alone, the US retailer offers more than 25 million titles in a variety of languages. It would be practically impossible to find books meeting one's requirements without the use of an intelligent search system organized by title, author, publisher, language, etc. This kind of system, however, amounts to little more than a simple catalogue, which will naturally be of assistance to consumers who already know what they want to buy and who simply need to locate it on the basis of certain well-defined criteria. But Amazon does much more than this. By keeping track of the search and buying patterns on its site, it is in a position to identify 'clusters' of interests and tag these to specific clients. Through the use of a buying list of this type, it can continually prompt customers with new titles which could be of interest but which could have escaped their attention. Fundamentally, the system simply labels the books in its catalogue with a variety of thematic groupings on the basis of readers' choices.

Let us suppose for instance that I purchase a text by author A and that a certain number of other clients do likewise. These clients in turn may buy books by authors B, C, D, etc. Should a pattern emerge whereby these customers also buy works by a further author, let us say F, then the system deduces that this author is in some way related by content to author A and hence will prompt me to purchase author F. As a regular book-buyer and reader, I can bear witness that the system works wonderfully. Even in areas where I have a good knowledge of the panorama of authors and output, the buying list is still able to surprise me by proposing titles and even authors I did not know and, almost invariably, they turn out to be apposite suggestions, and I will give serious consideration to making the purchase. In this manner, Amazon helps me not only to find items I am consciously seeking, but also those I would probably be interested in, if I was aware of them.

Could this be the solution to the paradox of choice? Only in part. In identifying a large number of titles possibly of interest to me, Amazon undoubtedly increases the number of alternatives amongst which I must choose, thus complicating my buying decision. On the other hand, the system's efficiency in identifying and proposing relevant titles effectively frees time and energy I would otherwise have to spend searching, and which I can now dedicate to choosing. The order in which new titles are submitted to my attention also facilitates the decision-making process. My impression at least is that these are ranked in order of possible relevance. In other words, the first screen of titles being proposed is typically more closely connected to my reading interests than the second, and so on.

Lastly – and for me this represents probably the most useful feature – Amazon also offers the option of saving a personal wish list of books which are of interest, but which the customer cannot or does not want to buy immediately. In this manner the need to choose is mitigated by the fact of being able to delay the purchase. Thus the trade-off between 'yes' or 'no' is transformed into 'now or later', to some extent attenuating the paradox of choice. This is because the purchase of a given book entails only a temporary rejection of other titles which we can decide to buy later, including them on the wish list which Amazon makes available to all registered users. This list is personalized, individualized, always available and update able. Adding a book to it amounts to almost taking possession of it, making it part of one's own pool of resources. Often, for example, I find myself examining my bookcase at home to see the titles I would like to try and read over the following weeks, and then immediately consulting my wish list to do exactly the same thing.

It is as if both of these constituted comparable ways of gaining access to books. It is true that in the latter case I cannot pick them up, leaf through them or of course read them. However, the first step – author, title and summary – is essentially the same, as are the respective feelings of possession and availability.

Does all this constitute an advantage for Amazon? Does the fact of granting this feeling of possession in miniature help the US retailer to sell books? In my case it certainly does, and for a number of reasons. In the first place the wish list acts as an historic memory in regard to the evolution of my interests in general and the embodiment of these in terms of specific books. In my list, for example, I can still find books that I registered 2 or 3 years ago, now wholly forgotten, connected perhaps with a particular theme that occupied my mind for a few weeks in relation to a specific need. Reacquainting me with such titles can generate for Amazon a genuine possibility that the book will be bought. Without this reminder process it would have been almost impossible these would have come to my mind and hence the resulting chance of a sale would have been practically non-existent. At a more unconscious level, the reappearance of the same title every time one consults the wish list acts as a sort of advertising prompt. It is as if the book continues to reveal itself, to speak, to remind one of its availability for purchase. A possible result of this is a decision to buy a book which has been on the list for a while, not so much in response to an immediate need, but rather as a sort of compensating mechanism of the type: 'It's been there a while, so I'll buy it and that way I'll have it'. In this case, the mini endowment effect deriving from the wish list is transformed into a full-scale desire which determines my willingness to buy the book in question.

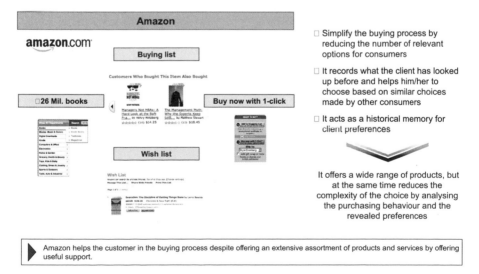

Figure 4.6   **The paradox of choice: does it generate the paradox or help to resolve it?**

Apple also uses a system of collective intelligence – i.e. of orientation to the tastes of individual users – to identify music or other media content of possible interest. The Genius system operates with iTunes, the Apple digital megastore offering an immense variety of music, films, TV programmes, podcasts and audio books. But Genius is also accessible from iPods, the app dedicated to the storage, listening and viewing of users' own music or videos. The interesting point here is that within iPod, the purpose of Genius is not to help people to identify music they like for online purchase, but simply to create playlists by selecting from users' existing collections, like a sort of personalized LP. Here it is not just a matter of helping consumers to find what they seek or what they might like from the potentially infinite selection available for online distribution. The idea is rather to aid listeners to find their way around their own collections of music.

It is true that the original idea behind Genius was probably more comparable to a sort of digital DJ which could make a sensible and enjoyable arrangement of one's own songs without the need for a physical person who could order the sequence of songs by changing LPs or CDs. But the continuous expansion of the music collections stored on people's computers or MP3 players created a problem of choice. When you possess hundreds – or indeed thousands – of songs and you wish to listen to them in a mixed sequence, without reference to their original albums, the selection and the sequencing can be a problem. The risk is that you end up always listening to the same ones because they are those that spring to mind, or that you jump around haphazardly, possibly spending more time choosing than really listening. In these circumstances, Genius helps to reduce the effort of making a selection, establishing on the basis of an initial choice of song a musical genre which the system refers to in selecting successive items on the playlist. Here is another intelligent system which, on the basis of predefined criteria, helps us to minimize the effort of making a choice and to enjoy to the full our experience as consumers.

CHAPTER 5

SUNK COSTS AND RE-EMERGING COSTS

Economic theory starts from the assumption that incremental costs alone influence the behaviour of consumers. Sunk costs are supposed to be irrelevant. Incremental costs are those costs which must be borne as a result of a given decision or action but not otherwise. Sunk costs on the other hand are those costs which have already been borne but which can no longer be recovered. Goods and services which have been bought but which can no longer be sold second-hand constitute a straightforward sunk cost corresponding to the original purchase price.

If for example we buy a non-refundable plane ticket from Milan to Rome, then our decision as to whether or not we should in fact fly to Rome should be influenced not by the fact of having already acquired the ticket, but solely by the utility and by the (additional) costs we face in going to Rome by plane or otherwise. Let us imagine, for instance, that at the time of leaving the bus connection to the airport is not running due a strike on the part of the drivers, and that the only real alternative to reach the airport is a taxi. Let us also imagine that in fact we could also go to Rome by train, which is an equally rapid and convenient way of travelling. The decision to take a taxi to get to the airport in order to get a plane to fly to Rome or to walk to the central station in order to take the train to travel to Rome should not be influenced by the fact of already having bought the air ticket, but simply by the comparison between the cost of the taxi and the cost of the train (Fig. 5.1).

5.1 THE COSTS OF THE PAST

In contrast with the claims of economic theory, the idea of sunk costs being irrelevant does not appear to correspond with the manner in which present decisions are influenced by past expenditure. In reality, the costs of the past count. In particular, we can say that other things being equal, the fact of paying for a product will increase the probability and the level of its usage.

Take the case of pricing models based on a flat-rate mechanism. This type of pricing, which is now very prevalent, is characterized by the fact that gaining access to the service involves the payment of a certain fixed cost, regardless of

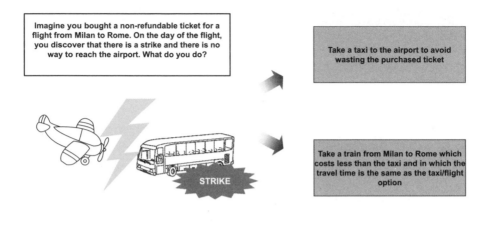

Imagine you bought a non-refundable ticket for a flight from Milan to Rome. On the day of the flight, you discover that there is a strike and there is no way to reach the airport. What do you do?

Take a taxi to the airport to avoid wasting the purchased ticket

STRIKE

Take a train from Milan to Rome which costs less than the taxi and in which the travel time is the same as the taxi/flight option

According to economic theory, only incremental costs affect consumer behaviour. So, the impact of sunk costs should be irrelevant.

Figure 5.1   The sunk costs effect: what is a rational consumer supposed to do?

the effective level of usage. Once this amount is paid, it becomes effectively a sunk cost in that it will not be reimbursed and does not vary in accordance with the real usage of the product. Classic examples include fixed rate unlimited calls telephone contracts, so-called 'eat as much as you like' deals in catering and free bank withdrawals from cash machines. Even subscriptions to newspapers and magazines can be interpreted as flat-rate deals: by paying a given sum of money at the beginning of the subscription period you get your own personal copy delivered, independently of whether the publication in question is read or not.

With these models what is generally found is a greater usage of the product in comparison with that associated with users of products with different pricing structures. Data traffic by flat-rate tariff users is higher, customers eat more in restaurants offering 'eat as much as you like' deals, and customers who do not pay for each withdrawal tend to use cash machines more frequently (especially if the deal includes withdrawals from other banks, thus removing the minor disincentive associated with having to walk a certain distance or take the car to reach a branch of one's own bank).

It is difficult to prove incontrovertibly that flat-rate pricing models prompt a higher usage of products, in so doing violating the principle of the irrelevance of sunk costs. For instance, the causal relationship could be the inverse: people who know they use the telephone a lot, eat a lot or need to make frequent cash withdrawals will be more likely to go for flat-rate deals in comparison with those who expect to have more limited and predictable patterns of consumption.

Certain indications can, however, be gleaned in relation to this question insofar as an identical product or service may be used more intensively by the same consumer after having passed to a flat-rate deal for the relevant product or service. Let us examine some examples.

I remember a holiday in London in my university days organized on a very limited budget, so limited that I had to watch even the money I spent on my daily meals. The strategy I adopted was as follows: during the week I ate very cheaply, using ingredients bought from the supermarket, then on Saturday evening I had a massive slap-up dinner at one of the numerous Indian restaurants offering 'eat as much as you like' menus. Certainly, the decision to go to these restaurants was motivated by the fact of having accumulated a certain hunger during the week. It is also true that after eating the first two or three courses my hunger tended to abate. But not, however, the greed provoked by the idea of being able to eat whatever I wanted 'for free'. And this was precisely where the logical error lay. It is not in fact true that I did not have to pay to eat that food, but just that I did not have to pay extra to do so. I am sure that the proprietors of the restaurants had already 'factored in' this extra into the original fixed price, thus making my feasts much less of a bargain than I imagined. Rather than the later courses being free, it was rather the first ones that cost more.

In the absence of concrete data it is difficult to establish if subscriptions cause an increase in the effective usage of newspapers, whether subscribers read more because they are subscribers or whether they are subscribers because they read more. However, it seems reasonable to suppose that that the constant physical availability of the newspaper in the home or the office would encourage people to read it out of simple convenience as well as out of a sort of uncomfortable sense of waste at seeing it thrown away unread the next day or the next week. This at least is what I feel when I don't find time to read the daily paper which arrives at my house or the weeklies and monthlies I subscribe to.

The fact that the subscription price for newspapers is often substantially lower than the news-stand price also seems to support an idea of increased use, or at least of increased sales. From an economic point of view, for publishers home delivery signifies saving on distribution costs in terms of the vendor's margin, although since this saving is quite modest it does not necessarily cover the cost of postage incurred with home delivery.

The discount applied to subscriptions should therefore be interpreted more in terms of publishers obtaining greater and more stable volumes. The decision of whether to buy the newspaper or not is reduced to a single act which will not later fall victim to lack of time or energy as in the case of the daily purchasing decision. Having obviated this possibility, because the newspaper will arrive at the home regardless of day-to-day circumstances and will be available for reading regardless of time or motivation and at no additional cost, simple convenience together with a feeling of duty will increase the chances of its being read.

It thus appears that a certain factor of self-selection on the part of clients operates in regard to flat-rate pricing models; but added to this is a phenomenon of disproportionally high usage resulting from the impression of being offered what economists term 'a free lunch', or in other words an asset for which no payment is necessary. How should this over-consumption be interpreted?

A first explanation certainly lies in the fact that there is effectively no marginal cost associated with such products, even when there is a decrease in marginal utility. When no additional expenditure is incurred by a further hour of Internet surfing, another spring roll or for reading more of the news, the consumer may decide to continue consuming the product even when the utility of the extra hour's surfing, spring roll or news information is very low. In theory the consumer could continue to consume until the point where doing so becomes a sacrifice and only then would he stop.

In some situations, however, there are additional costs associated with continued use of a product which may be of a collateral nature rather than in terms of direct payment for the product itself. Excessive use of the Internet may for example have negative physical side-effects (e.g. for the eyesight) or psychological ones (alienation from reality), while it will certainly take away from time available for other activities. In the restaurant situation the knowledge that eating as much

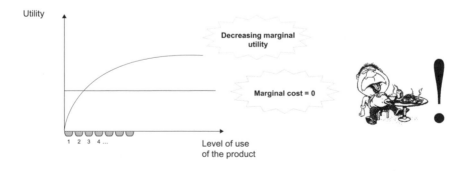

The consumer may decide to purchase additional units of the product simply because they're free of charge, even if the utility of the last unit was very low.

Figure 5.2   The sunk costs effect: if it's for free, why shouldn't we take it?

as you like, beyond a certain limit, can lead to the risk of getting a bad case of indigestion or spending the night awake with heartburn is a good example of the costs incurred by further consumption of the product. And yet we still keep eating. Just to read the newspaper because it's paid for can mean depriving oneself of other, possibly more worthwhile activities such as playing with one's children or talking to one's wife (Fig. 5.2).

5.2 FUTURE LOSSES

Another possible explanation for the importance of sunk costs could be that the consumer transforms them, in some subconscious manner, into opportunity costs. Such a psychological mechanism could be what induces the consumer to interpret the non-use or non-consumption of an asset which has already been paid for as some kind of missed opportunity. Since the dessert is included in the price, I'll try it. Even if I have just sent an email to my colleague, I'll call him – after all, it's free. It's a pity to throw away the paper without even opening it, although I don't really feel like it today. The positive hedonistic principle can thus correspond to the pleasure of getting a bargain, and the negative hedonistic principle to that of avoiding a loss (Fig. 5.3).

The pricing models used for example in telecoms, in the world of finance, in catering and in publishing are all characterized by an initial cost which gives access to the product and which influences the consumer while violating the principle of sunk costs. Technically these are referred to as flat-rate models. There are other

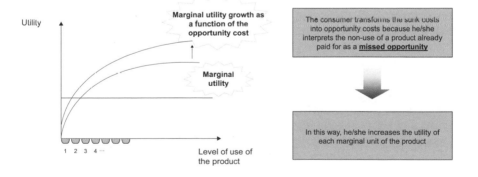

The consumer automatically transforms the sunk costs into opportunity costs because he/she interprets the non-use of a product already paid for as a missed opportunity.

Figure 5.3   The sunk costs effect: am I losing out on an opportunity?

models, however, in which the up-front payment is not the only form of charge, but where additional fees are levied which vary with the actual use of the product. In this case we can speak of 'multipart pricing' (Thaler 1980). A classic example is that of the tennis club where payment of the annual membership fee confers the right of booking the courts, which will then be paid for separately on the basis of usage.

In the flat-rate model, price variations will have an impact on purchasing volumes in keeping with the law of supply and demand. An increase in the price will lead to a decrease in the number of people willing to buy the product, while lowering it will increase the number. In the multi-part model, a price increase will also reduce the actual usage of the service in line with the income effect. This is because the higher price required initially to join the club will consume resources the member would otherwise have spent on hiring courts during the year. Hence, in this case, an increase in the membership fee will have a knock-on effect in reducing overall usage of the courts belonging to the club: a reduction in the number of users arising from the law of demand, together with a fall in levels of usage due to the income effect (Fig. 5.4).

The considerations examined above in regard to sunk costs give rise to a further reflection, however. This is that these will act as a counterweight to the income

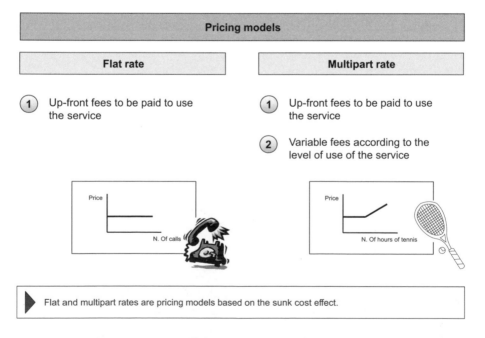

Flat and multipart rates are pricing models based on the sunk cost effect.

Figure 5.4   The sunk costs effect: what are the consequences for business?

effect, tending to increase the hire of the courts where the income effect tends to decrease it. The same can be said in regard to additional and unexpected psychological costs at the time of purchase. Take the example of the regular tennis player who continues to play even when affected by tennis elbow. Thaler (1985) observes that the payment of the initial club subscription fee could greatly increase usage, precisely because not to play would represent a waste. I could not agree more (Fig 5.5).

I well recall a man of about 50, a long-time member of the tennis club where I played as a child, who arrived at the court one day with a heavily bandaged arm due to a case of tennis elbow. Hanging from it was a bag containing transparent liquid which looked like water. Leaving the court, another member asked him what he had on his arm and what was in the bag. The reply was bewildering: 'I have shooting pains in my arm but I don't want to stop playing. I've tried creams, massages, ointments, everything, but it just won't go. A friend brought me this from Lourdes, we'll see if it helps.' This surely was a case where sunk costs continued to weigh greatly on his decision-making.

Even if it is difficult to demonstrate theoretically which of the two factors will prevail, it is nevertheless clear that they will have opposing influences such that the higher the price for access to the product, the greater the sunk costs effect will be and the resulting usage that customers will make of the product in question. Conversely, the higher the buying price, the fewer the number of people who will be willing to buy the product (firstly) and (secondly) the lower the level of usage, in accordance with the correlation between demand and the income effect.

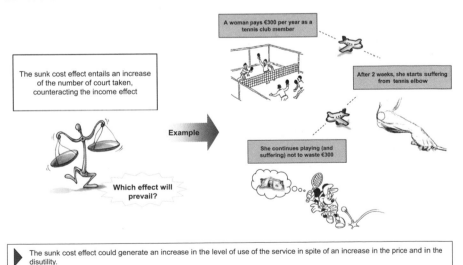

Figure 5.5   The sunk costs effect: can it counteract the decrease in volumes?

5.3 THE PAST THAT PASSES

Although sunk costs will influence later decisions, this process will not continue ad infinitum. Indeed it seems logical that their effects on behaviour should be limited in time. The frequency with which season ticket holders go to the theatre will be very high in the period immediately following their acquiring the season ticket and will tend to diminish thereafter. My experience after the purchase of my first theatre season ticket as a student confirms this. The pricing structure was as follows: the payment of a fixed sum conferred the right to receive tickets for six performances during the season. This price was 30 per cent lower than the total I would have paid to buy the tickets singly. However, the seats assigned were not always in the best positions and not all of the most interesting productions were included, hence the lower price. When I had purchased the season ticket, my enthusiasm for this adventure into theatre was high, as was my willingness to adapt to these constraints. After a few months, however, the shows seemed increasingly less suited to my needs and my other commitments increasingly difficult to manage, with the result that the last of the tickets stayed in the drawer.

An aside: in Chapter 7 on mental accounting we will see how often the amount we are willing to spend for a given item depends on how it is classified among the various categories of expenditure. Spending money on the theatre for example can be classified as simple enjoyment or as an investment in one's cultural development. In the latter case, other factors being equal, the motivation to invest money is likely to increase, basically because the expenditure is for an important end – i.e. our own selves and our capacity to appreciate the 'finer' things of life.

This type of argument can naturally also be used in seeking to convince others and in persuading them to support us in such a venture. And this is exactly what took place at the time with my father. Presenting the request for a season ticket to him as a great step forward in my maturity and a concrete proof of my interest in something other than motorbikes and discotheques, I led him to take a view of this request as being something different from the normal fad or impulse of the moment. The season ticket thus presented me with the opportunity to enjoy six extra evenings out, paid for outside the normal agreed monthly allowance, while my father could say to himself in absolute good faith that it was money well spent. To be honest I am not sure it was.

CHAPTER 6

DIVIDE AND RULE

In the previous chapter we analysed a number of cases in which sunk costs affected purchase and usage decisions regarding products. In this chapter we look at the topic of payment, analysing and focusing on the importance of the timing stages between these three phases in a transaction. The flat-rate model used in telecoms, where normally the use of the service for a month is followed by the payment of the fixed monthly tariff, represents a form of post-paid contract in which the purchasing decision precedes the usage decision and the payment decision. By contrast, the enrolment at the tennis club corresponds to a form of pre-paid contract, in the sense that acquisition and payment of the one-off subscription fee take place at the beginning of the year, to be followed by the use of the service over the following 12 months. Economic theory sustains that this time lapse between the moments of buying, using and paying for something play a role because of 'the time value of money'. The behavioural approach adds some interesting ideas to this, in some cases providing for the inverse effect to what classical economic theory would assume. Let us examine this in more detail.

6.1 PAYING, BUYING AND USING

The first case considered by economic theory can be labelled as the risk of unavailability. The idea here is that gaining access to an asset today avoids the risk of not being able to do so in the future. If a product is available in a limited quantity and there is the risk that soon it will no longer be found on the market, a consumer would immediately be willing to make a purchasing and payment decision, even though he or she does not intend to use the product straightaway. In this case risk aversion leads to the purchase or pushes the consumer in that direction. The second situation in which, according to economic theory, a time dimension affects purchasing dynamics is capitalization. In this case, purchasing a product allows you to enjoy the benefits of using it immediately. Even though, in principle, such dynamics apply to all products, money plays a special role here. The idea is that possessing a certain amount of money will allow you to invest it and earn returns and such returns will allow you to increase the amount of your money over time. In these cases we speak of capitalization. At the same time, keeping your money means avoiding the risk of someone else misusing it and losing it. In such cases, we refer to risk aversion. These are the two reasons why we expect to earn interest when we lend capital or expect a discount when we pay in advance. The time between purchase, use and payment of a product is therefore a key factor because, other things being equal, it is better to purchase and consume before rather than after, while paying afterwards is better than paying before.

Often, however, what is observed is an influence deriving from the separation of these two phases which goes beyond normal expectations in terms either of possible capitalization or risk in relation to the asset to be acquired. Let us take the example of credit cards. It seems clear that the fact of being able to separate the moment of acquisition from that of payment increases levels of expenditure to a degree which is not justified by the fact that payment is delayed on average by a month. If this were not the case, shopkeepers would be unlikely to accept paying commissions on transactions, commissions which can amount to 1–2 per cent of the value of card payments. A much more compelling explanation for the influence (in terms of willingness to spend) of the separation between the moment of payment and that of consumption is that this seems to reduce the attention given to the cost of the product thus acquired.

Soman (2001) has demonstrated how such a time lapse will undoubtedly exert an influence on our buying patterns, even if acting in combination with a series of other psychological mechanisms. In 1997 the University of Toronto researcher stopped 41 students coming out of a campus bookstore after having made a purchase. The students were asked what method of payment they had used and to name the sum they had just spent. By cross-checking with each student's receipts, Soman was able to deduce that 12 out of 18 students (66.7 per cent) who had paid in cash remembered exactly how much they had paid, with the remaining 6 under or overestimating the sum by a maximum of $3. Among those who had paid by credit card, on the other hand, only 8 out of 23 (34.8 per cent) were able to remember the exact amount, while the other 15 cited a figure lower than the sum really paid or confessed to not having the slightest idea.

The experiment shows that the actual mental registration of expenditure is subject to considerable variation depending on the means of payment. This in turn suggests that the means of payment can influence the prominence given to the sacrifice associated with the payment. The obvious consequence of this is that, for a given product and price, our willingness to spend will increase if the payment is made by credit card. Needless to say, this phenomenon can equally be explained by reference to the non-physical and unlimited nature of card payments. Taking out bank notes and seeing them disappear into the hands of the cashier might easily appear more painful than making a simple signature. Likewise, the combined value of banknotes we carry with us will normally be lower than the limit on a credit card and this alone can modify our willingness to spend. Nevertheless, the fact that purchases made via credit card will introduce a time-lag between the moment of acquiring goods and that of paying for them (i.e. the 'sacrifice') will probably be an equally important factor, especially in the light of the problems relating to self-control which will be examined in Chapter 8.

There are at least four ways in which the use of credit cards separates the phases of acquisition and of payment, all of which are relevant in explaining the generalized increase in willingness to spend (Thaler 1980). In the narrowest sense, the use of cards allows the cash-strapped consumer to bring forward purchases by a month or so, or vice versa to delay the relevant payments. We have already seen how this might have an economic effect. Secondly, by substituting a signature for a cash payment, credit cards downplay the act of paying, thus rendering it less unacceptable. The ability to exceed the limit represented by the amount of cash we have in our wallet through the use of cards is a further factor tending to increase expenditure. Lastly, there is also the fact that when the credit card statement arrives at the end of the month, the various prices will all appear mixed up in the list of transactions, thereby making it more difficult to stigmatize individual purchases. The fact of having spent €100 for a bottle of perfume, for example, will be overshadowed by a number of other purchases of similar dimensions, and even more so in the context of a total expenditure many times greater. The €100 then becomes one item among many and will appear relatively minor in relation to the total. To what degree the spending of for example €2,000 will be unacceptable to a given consumer depends on his personal propensity to consume as well as naturally on his budget constraints, in the sense of the financial resources at his disposal. On the other hand, the difficulty of dividing the unpleasantness associated with an overall cost, whether great or small, between individual items of expenditure, is a general problem. As one might say, it is easy to identify the crime, but difficult to identify the real culprit. Moreover, let us not forget that all these effects will tend to be magnified if the credit card bill is paid only in part through a revolving mechanism which will further extend the time-lag between consumption and payment.

6.2 PAYING AND SECURING

The separation of payment from usage can also generate a kind of insurance effect. This might include for example not ruining a pleasant telephone conversation by associating it directly with the cost of the call. I believe this represents one of the real reasons which lead many telephone customers to choose a flat-rate deal, even when paying per call would be cheaper. For a person using the phone, not having to think about meter ticking or the minutes passing can in fact generate value and consequently a greater willingness to spend. Naturally, here too the point made in earlier chapters will apply, regarding the phenomenon of self-selection among users opting for certain pricing models. In many cases consumers who know that they make frequent use of the telephone will be oriented towards a flat-rate tariff as a result. A clear causal relationship between the two cannot necessarily be established, however. Many consumers choose flat-rate deals so as not to have to think any longer about telephone costs. This security takes on a value in itself, and in turn influences the frequency and duration of calls.

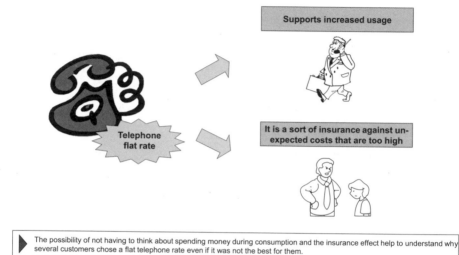

The possibility of not having to think about spending money during consumption and the insurance effect help to understand why several customers chose a flat telephone rate even if it was not the best for them.

Figure 6.1   The separation effect: can I relax?

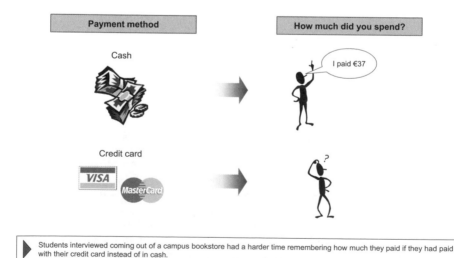

Students interviewed coming out of a campus bookstore had a harder time remembering how much they paid if they had paid with their credit card instead of in cash.

Figure 6.2   The separation effect: can I remember how much I spent?

The insurance effect plays a further role, which is to align the interests of the payer with those of the consumer. I remember when my sister and I were both teenagers, beginning to discover the vital importance of spending at least two hours a day on the phone with our friends to exchange real-time updates on the latest TV series, to give and receive help with homework assignments, or just to say that we would be in touch later by phone (the so-called 'second level' calls!). In that period my father was literally terrified when the time came to open the telephone bill. I am certain that he would have willingly paid a flat-rate premium in order to be certain in advance that the costs of his children's communicative frenzy could go beyond a certain limit (Fig. 6.2).

6.3 PAYING AND MISALLOCATING

In many cases there will be a crossover between the behavioural impact of the twin phenomena of sunk costs examined in the last chapter and the separation between payment and consumption discussed above. Let us take the case of the car. Many city-dwellers would gain a substantial economic advantage by doing without ownership of a car in favour of a combined use of bicycles, the underground system, taxis and car hire. This was in fact the strategy I adopted in my early years living in Munich, a city which is extremely well-organized in terms of cycle paths, public transport, affordable taxis and of course car hire options both in regard to the range of cars offered and ease of access. The way I approached the question was as follows: for normal journeys I took the bike or the underground (depending on the time available) while for one-off needs I took a taxi (for example during a Saturday night out); the option of renting a car was reserved for special needs (such as a trip to IKEA) or for weekends in the mountains or at the lake. After 10 years or so when my financial situation had improved I decided to buy a car. In view of the fact that I lived in the centre while my work as a consultant normally involves travel by train or by plane, the car was normally kept in the garage five days out of seven and thus did not make a significant difference to my mode of travel. The only real difference it made was in the number of weekends away. But why was this?

From a purely economic point of view, the purchase of the car should in theory have reduced the number of weekends away, for the simple reason that the cost of the car would reduce the total resources available for leisure. However, from a psychological viewpoint, the fact of having a car reduced the cost of each single trip away. The separation between the moment of paying for the car and the organization of my weekends led me to view these as being less extravagant, thus making them more attractive and increasing their frequency as a result. From an economically rational angle, this amounted to simply transforming a variable cost into a fixed cost, so that I (mistakenly) ceased to include the cost of the car in the cost of the weekend. The overall running costs of the car (hire purchase payments, petrol, insurance and maintenance) were, however, substantially increased. It may be true that the motoring costs per weekend were lower insofar as the number of outings was greater, but the paradox lies in the fact that the increase in the number of trips was based on the misconception of a lower cost for each trip, which could not in fact be the case.

The transformation of variable costs into fixed costs and their mistaken allocation nevertheless represent only a partial explanation of the 'private car' phenomenon. A further contributing element is the fact that, on a psychological level, the car, once bought, conforms to the mechanism of sunk and re-emerging costs examined in the last chapter. In the period following the purchase, the ownership of the car is taken for granted and no consideration is given to the idea of selling it. In this sense it represents less an opportunity cost than a sunk cost. In the meantime, the fact of having it available in the garage for Sunday outings induces us to make use of it for that end. We do this because not to do so would be a waste. The car thus represents once again a sort of opportunity cost, not, however, in the economic sense of a fixed investment which cannot be used differently but rather in the sense of an option which is to hand and which it would be a pity not to exploit. The mind of the consumer no longer thinks in terms of opportunity costs as such, but much more in terms of opportunities missed.

6.4 PAYING AND SELF-BINDING

We have seen that economic theory assumes that it is generally preferable to acquire and to consume a product before paying for it. This order of preferences can be attributed to the categories of risk and of capitalization. In the course of this chapter, however, we have at various points also seen that the time lapse between purchase, payment and use can have effects which differ from the predictions of the theory of 'time value of money'. Some kinds of transaction can even be interpreted in the opposite manner, where it is assumed that it is preferable to bring forward the payment and delay the consumption.

Richard Thaler uses the example of the now very widespread model of the all-inclusive holiday resort village. The principle underlying this success is that the client pays for the whole holiday in advance thereby acquiring, as it were, a sort of insurance policy in regard to the overall cost. In paying this initial sum, the consumer knows that he will be able to make use of a vast array of extra services, which will include for example sporting activities and facilities such as swimming pools or gyms, entertainment, recreation and baby-sitting, as well as a range of food, drinks, lounges, beaches, and so on. The basic idea is that the client can stop thinking about money and not be influenced in his decision whether or not to make use of any service by considerations of cost. The hedonistic mechanism is not having any worries, as expressed in the slogan: pay the price in your travel agency and leave your wallet at home.

☐ Clients don't have to think about money

☐ They avoid single transactions being more expensive than expected (bargaining effect)

☐ There is no link with real money as "fake" money is used

**Resort
All-inclusive**

▶ Separating payment and consumption seems to reduce the perceived cost of using the product bought in this way.

Figure 6.3   The separation effect: why do people choose to relax in resort villages?

Similarly, many gyms charge monthly or even yearly subscriptions, avoiding pricing models based on effective usage. This mechanism likewise separates consumption from payment, making the marginal cost of a visit equal to zero. The monthly charge encourages consumption on the part of those wishing to reduce the cost per visit or get the best value for money spent. This model can also be helpful for potentially under-consuming clients, such as those who would like to attend the gym regularly but have reason to fear that they will not in fact do so, whether for lack of time or out of laziness. The pre-pay system will help these people in two different ways. First, by making each single visit appear free, thus eliminating one of the possible excuses used by the lazy punter – i.e. not wishing or not being able to spend the money. A pay-per-use pricing system (piece rate pricing), on the other hand, would underline the connection between the act of consumption and payment, thus diminishing the utility: quite apart from not desiring to go to the gym, I would also have to pay. Second, acting through the psychological mechanism of sunk and re-emerging costs, the flat-rate pricing model creates a strong incentive to use the gym as much as possible in order not to miss the opportunity for free use associated with the purchase of the subscription.

Also those situations in which the potential buyer expects some reduction in the resources at his disposal over the intervening interval could increase the attractiveness of the 'pay first, consume later' pricing model. In these cases, aware of the fact that the money could be soon gone, the consumer prefers to advance the payment thus avoiding any possibility of spending it in another way. The client of the gym might for example be happy to pay the annual membership fee at the beginning of the year, because at that moment he still has money left over from his bonus, which, if not used for the membership fees, would be spent on other things in the following months. In a manner which is almost the diametrical opposite to the capitalization of money, here the key aspect is being able to advance the money at a time when one is certain of having resources available, resources which could be subject to dispersion with the passage of time, especially in the light of the many uncertainties relating to self-control and to budget limitations.

CHAPTER 7

MONEY GAMES

In principle, the source of money should not influence its value in our eyes. For example, €100 earned by working has the same value as €100 won in the lottery. If I am disposed to spend €100 for a match ticket, I will be so regardless of whether I won or earned the sum. The underlying economic conception is that the €100 will contribute to our overall level of wealth, on the basis of which we will decide if the cost of the ticket is greater than the utility derived from seeing the game. If this is judged to be greater than utility we can expect from an alternative use of the money then we will buy the ticket, while otherwise we will not do so – naturally with the proviso that our economic circumstances are such that we can afford it, i.e. that the purchase falls within what economists term our budget constraints (Fig. 7.1).

7.1 FORM BECOMES SUBSTANCE

The make-up of our overall wealth should constitute a neutral factor with regard to our spending behaviour. The way that money is conserved or invested ought not in fact to influence our purchasing decisions. Money sitting in our current account should be spent – or not spent – in an identical manner to that invested in a long-term savings plan. Leaving aside the constraints on liquidity or withdrawal (since money in a current account is available at any moment from the bank, the cash machine or via credit/debit card, while gaining access to money from an investment plan generally requires a more complicated procedure frequently involving delays and/or penalty clauses), making use of money from the current account or from the investment plan should make absolutely no difference. This is because according to economic theory money is money, i.e. a unit of exchange which is absolutely convertible or tradable and which has neither category nor label.

The consequence is that our willingness to spend for a specific item should likewise not be determined by any type of categorization or preconception regarding the manner of its acquisition. The purchase is decided by reference to a calculation of the item's utility, the financial resources available and the asking price. If these factors are in the appropriate relation, the purchase will take place, regardless of the means of payment or the pricing model. Here again the basic idea is that

According to economic theory, the source of money does not affect its value

▶ €100 obtained working should have the same value as €100 won in the lottery.

Figure 7.1   Mental accounting: what is a rational consumer supposed to do?

the consumer performs a rational evaluation of the advantages and disadvantages associated with the opportunity and on that basis decides whether or not to proceed.

Precisely this fungible (exchangeable) quality of money is at the heart of life-cycle theory, probably the most widely accepted economic theory relating to the movements of money and the structuring of assets. It was developed by the Italian Franco Modigliani, winner of the 1985 Nobel Prize for Economics. The theory starts from the assumption that individuals throughout their lives calibrate their patterns of consumption in such a way as to obtain the greatest possible benefit with no thought to leaving wealth to their heirs. In order to calculate their level of consumption for any given year they should ascertain the present value of their income – taking into account factors of risk and impatience – together with projected future income and net accumulated assets, regardless of source or composition. The resulting figure should be used to purchase an annuity – a financial instrument which, in exchange for an up-front payment of a substantial sum of money, will guarantee an annual return for life. The individual's level of consumption should thereafter correspond exactly to this amount year by year, so as to maximize the overall utility of consumption, while leaving nothing to future generations.

While it might be very elegant and precisely applicable in regard to problems of optimization, life-cycle theory does not seem to show much correspondence to empirical reality. As Thaler (1992) underlines in his broad overview of empirical studies dedicated to this question, in the first place it does not appear correct that the level of consumption remains stable over the years. On the contrary, it shows a strong correlation with current income levels. Young people tend to consume too little with regard to their expected earnings, middle-aged people too much in relation to their actual earnings and the elderly once again consume too little, especially in view of the property wealth they have accumulated over time. Even on a yearly basis, changes in consumption levels show a strong correlation with disposable income thus diverging from the model of the stabilization of consumption over time. Essentially, it appears that the inclination of young people to take on debt is lower than the level assumed by the life-cycle theory, as is old people's inclination to cash in on and spend the patrimony accumulated during their lives.

Such anomalies with regard to the predictions of Modigliani's theory have naturally received considerable attention from economists who have offered a number of differing explanations. A first hinges on the concept of limited rationality. Even if the optimization of expenditure in the light of income and current wealth may seem a straightforward question from a theoretical point of view, very often people have neither the inclination nor the time, or even the ability, to pursue this line of reasoning. Forecasting the variations of future income, identifying a discount rate which can assign a sensible current value to these and buying a suitable investment plan capable of generating the appropriate payments over time is anything but a simple task.

While very sensible and also intuitive, the limitation of this explanation is that if this were really the method used by individuals to manage their income and consumption over time, then the market would have provided appropriate instruments to resolve the various difficulties of planning and of calculation. And sure enough dozens of software packages and applications are in existence which can help consumers to manage their finances, not to mention the services of professional financial consultants available even to those with limited capital to invest. In other words, a pretty broad range of technological and professional assistance can be drawn on to resolve the problems of optimization posed by the life-cycle theory. However, demand for and use of such products and services does not seem to match the supply as would be necessary to meet the requirements of the theory itself in terms of optimization.

An alternative explanation essentially calls into question the assumption that the reference time frame for the distribution of consumption is the lifetime of the individual with the exclusion of possible successors. From the point of view of a non-economist such an assumption does indeed seem rather extreme. Just think of the behaviour of the vast majority of relatives in our experience – be they parents, uncles and aunts, grandparents and so on – but also of the standard value proposition associated with private banking, which is generally more concerned with the conserving, maintaining and safeguarding of assets than with their growth or liquidation. In the same way, think of the advertising messages associated with certain luxury or collector's goods, such as the Patek Philippe slogan: 'You never actually own a Patek Philippe, you merely look after it for the next generation.' Such examples show a clear orientation to future generations. The concept of 'inheritance', in contrast with the theory of life cycles, thus appears to possess greater intuitive and persuasive force, although probably it tells only part of the story.

In an interesting article concerning the behaviour of elderly people with regard to their property portfolio, Venti and Wise (1989) note that the tendency to sell properties in order to increase consumption is indeed low and also – crucially in relation to the role of successors – that this remains essentially unvaried for families with or without children. It is true that there are in reality other possible heirs, be they nephews, nieces, friends or charitable bodies, but these should normally exert a lesser influence on patterns of saving and consumption when compared to the desire to make arrangements for one's own children. That elderly property-owners tend normally not to sell, regardless of whether or not they have direct heirs, thus throws doubt on the notion that this type of behaviour can be explained simply by reference to the inclusion of future generations in one's own utility function and in the propensity to consume here and now.

Yet another explanation asserts that in reality individuals would be prepared to take out loans in order to stabilize their consumption levels. Often, however, they are not able to do this simply because no appropriate forms of financial package are available on the market. There is some truth in this theory. What is certain is that a sizeable proportion of loan requests which are refused relates to those (including young people) who wish simply to bring forward the moment of consumption on the basis of expected future revenues. Nevertheless, a multitude of financial instruments are available which have the precise function of transforming future wealth into present consumption – the whole consumer credit industry being an example – and these generally work by accepting future earnings as collateral, thus foregoing the guarantee of existing accumulated assets.

While such arguments will have a certain relevance in explaining the basic anomalies in the life-cycle theory, they do not tell the whole story. Or rather, the basic problem underlying the non-transposition of money and expenditure over time is more clearly revealed if we simply consider that in reality there exist forms of money which are not interchangeable. In essence, the origin of our money, our means of managing it and the circumstances in which we use it play a fundamental role, radically transforming our willingness to spend or save and consequently also our willingness to shift this in time in order to stabilize consumption.

First and foremost, it is anything but true that the origin of money is a neutral factor with regard to spending decisions. Generally speaking, money possessed or earned through great sacrifice will be spent less willingly than sums obtained unexpectedly or fortuitously. At the same time, sums which are small in relation to our present wealth are spent more easily than larger amounts. In a study conducted by Landsberger (1966) on the use of sums received in war reparations from Germany on the part of 297 Jewish families, a strong correlation was observed between the level of income, the amount received and the propensity to consume this money. In particular, families who had received a substantial payment (corresponding to around 60 per cent of their annual income) tended to consume a quarter of the amount and to save the rest. Families for whom the payment represented a small part of annual income (around 7 per cent) tended to spend excessively, sometimes doubling the figure, perhaps in order to form the necessary capital to acquire a certain asset.

The exceptional nature of a given inflow of money can also strongly influence the manner in which we spend it. I remember for example when I was 17 years old deciding to sell my electric guitar to a family friend, who wished to purchase it together with other classmates as a gift to another girl who was particularly popular. In comparison to the sum I had originally paid and to my expectation of a possible selling price, the friend's offer was extremely attractive. In no way did I expect to be able to obtain such a sum and as a result I was more than enthusiastic. It amounted – at least to my mind – to money growing on trees. And that is exactly how it was spent. In no time the money was finished, spent in a manner which was highly extravagant if compared to my normal approach with my modest weekly allowance. Something similar often affects people who have won sums of money in the lottery or at the casino, sums which are large enough to allow a one-off indulgence such as a nice dinner out or a purchase, but not enough to allow a lasting transformation of spending habits.

The make-up of assets also appears to influence people's propensity to consumption and hence their willingness to spend. The financial services industry offers innumerable alternative ways of placing money and of structuring one's investments, each characterized by differing rates of return and risk factors. Savers who invest money in shares will normally be prepared to accept the risk of seeing their savings shrink or even vanish completely in exchange for the chance of a good return. On the other hand, those who buy bonds (especially those issued by the German Treasury) will be happy with a very low or even negative yield, in return for the virtual certainty of being able to maintain the nominal value of their investments. Another perspective from which to view these savings and investment products relates to the ease and timescale of gaining access to the assets in order to transform them into liquidity. In the light of this criterion we can distinguish four categories of investment or ways of allocating resources.

Current assets are those which are immediately available at all times, corresponding essentially to cash and current account deposits. *Liquid assets* are those which can be converted within a few days or even hours, because they are held in forms or markets where it is possible at any time to find a buyer willing to purchase them. Typical examples include bonds, shares and investment funds. A third category is that of real estate assets, made up of buildings and land.

Although there can be broad variations depending on specific cases, the conversion of these types of asset will normally take longer. Their value cannot be precisely determined at any given moment (and can in fact be the end-result of a process of personal negotiation) and their sale or purchase involves going through more complicated bureaucratic and administrative procedures, such as notary acts and land registry formalities, than is required for the buying and selling of shares. Lastly, there are *pension assets* such as state pensions, private pension plans, severance pay and so on, which are normally accessible only at a given future moment and only subject to certain conditions, at risk of incurring the partial or complete loss of the asset in question.

The more difficult and laborious the process of gaining access to these types of assets, the less will be the temptation to spend the money invested in them. Given similar levels of overall wealth and preferences, the make-up of people's investments will therefore have an influence on their spending decisions. For example, while I may be willing to spend €3,000 for a TV if I have this sum in my current account, I might be reluctant to do so if it involves selling shares. Transaction costs and release times can therefore have a bearing on my buying patterns, thus belying the idea that my patterns of purchase are independent of the make-up of my assets.

The interesting point here is that, on the contrary, consumer behaviour with regard to such limitations is frequently the opposite of that posited by rational economic theory. In reality, the calculation performed by the consumer is designed to work within the limitations and constraints associated with the various types of assets so as to control and manage consumption over time, rather than to access all these sources of funds in order to maintain a constant level of consumption. The basic difference is that in the life-cycle theory it is assumed (through the operation of what we have defined as the concept of fungibility of money) that current income, net assets and expected future earnings will be managed in an identical manner, with a view to determining a constant level of consumption over time. The idea is that of interconnecting vessels where financial resources, like liquids, will automatically exploit mechanisms of discount and capitalization in order to find a common level (of consumption). However, the typical consumer appears to treat these three different types of asset in a completely different manner, following completely different patterns of spending behaviour according to the type of assets in question and – possibly even more importantly – actively selecting certain types of investment and assets rather than others precisely on the basis of their impact on purchasing and saving patterns.

7.2 THE ORIGIN OF MONEY

An interesting example of the role played by the origin of money in spending behaviour is the differing psychological attitudes to dividends and capital gains. Thaler (1980) observes that many companies seek to maintain a steady pattern of dividend payments over time, despite the fact that in countries such as the United States it would be preferable from the point of view of tax efficiency to reward shareholders through share buybacks, so boosting the share price. In the United States dividends attract a higher rate of taxation than capital gains and this means that for any given gross added value, the payment of dividends means distributing a lower net value in comparison with what could be obtained by the sale of shares at a higher corresponding price. So what is the reason for this?

One possible explanation is that savers like dividends because they provide an excellent protection against excessive spending or the excessively rapid consumption of assets. Dividends reduce this risk by encouraging the adoption of a very simple criterion: spend the dividends but don't touch the capital. Investors no longer need worry about tracking the overall state of their investment portfolio in relation either to the nominal value (i.e. the increase or decrease in capitalization of the shares held) or to the real value (i.e. in relation to inflation). All that is required is the separation of the current state of the portfolio from the associated cash flow and the limiting of expenditure to the latter.

The increase in overall wealth deriving from a rise in share prices is therefore perceived as different from the growth in current account deposits resulting from the payment of dividends. The vessel containing shares is thus not perfectly connected with that containing current account deposits, so that the destination of dividends can play a fundamental role in our propensity to spend.

A consumer who had no problems of self-control could thus afford to have a perfectly neutral attitude with regard to the formula adopted for the payment of dividends. If these were paid in cash he could simply use his current account in order to spend the desired amount. Similarly, however, he could sell an appropriate quota of shares in order to raise an amount equivalent to the missing dividends and spend the proceeds in the same manner. However, to start selling shares may be considered risky, especially for a consumer who does not wholly trust his own capacity for self-control or who possibly considers himself somewhat impulsive. There is in fact a genuine risk of giving in to temptation and being drawn into types of reasoning such as: 'Perhaps I could sell a few more shares and buy myself that watch I saw in the window last week instead of waiting until Christmas' or 'The shares are doing really well and so I won't need to hold many in my portfolio to pay back my loan at the expiry date.'

The fact of organizing one's investments in such a way that the associated added value is channelled into a form perceived as highly liquid (the current account) rather than into a form perceived as being less accessible and more inflexible (securities) can therefore have an influence on the use of these resources. In turn, the expectation of such usage can influence the value which the consumer assigns to the product. In the case of shares there are investors whose decisions regarding the allocation of capital will be strongly oriented towards shares paying regular dividends, thus investing in companies (in other words purchasing their capital 'product') on the precise basis of their dividend policy. This happens despite the fact that, from a viewpoint of pure financial efficiency, in actual fact this strategy is completely irrelevant or even negative, as we saw above, in terms of tax efficiency.

Returning to the structuring of assets – the way in which money is allocated – let us examine the effect this has on propensity to consume. An example is the Christmas savings scheme. Invented in the United States in 1909, this product met with considerable success for a period of years, until the invention of the credit card (1929) reduced the attractiveness of its value proposition. The basic idea behind this form of deposit account was simple. Over the course of the year most consumers would have access to sums of money which, if saved, would be enough to cover the costs of Christmas gifts they wished to purchase in the months of November and December.

This was exactly the problem: these sums were spread out through the course of the year, which represented a long period of time in which Christmas was still a remote prospect and the temptation to make alternative purchases could easily make itself felt, leading to a problem of self-control. A mindful consumer could nevertheless deal with the problem by investing regular sums in the Christmas savings scheme, which imposed a penalty on premature withdrawals while offering an interest rate only marginally greater than that paid on a current account.

It is difficult to explain the existence, let alone the success of such a product by reference to the theory of the rational consumer or to life-cycle theory. Why would a consumer sacrifice liquidity without receiving in return an improved return on his capital? An economic agent able to determine a precise level of desired expenditure and intending to stabilize his consumption through the movement of past or future resources in time, would logically take care to allocate these resources in such a manner as to maximize his potential returns in the context of existing constraints.

The Christmas savings scheme does exactly the opposite: it yields a limited return and imposes high barriers to exit, thus considerably restricting the investor's room for manoeuvre. But this is precisely what gives the product its appeal. Consumers, conscious of the risk of arriving at Christmas without the funds needed to purchase the necessary gifts, turn to this form of investment as a kind of safety barrier which forces them to curb their spending. Seen in this light, it is clear that the allocation of funds is anything but neutral with regard to our spending patterns, but that we consciously place money in a certain way precisely because we are aware that this will facilitate the adoption of certain forms of behaviour in preference to others.

I remember an event which took place a few years ago which is significant in this context. I had just moved to Germany and I needed to open a current account. In view of my limited fluency in the language at that time I had asked my German teacher to come with me so as to help me to understand at least the essential points in regard to conditions, costs and so on. At the bank, discussions proceeded fairly smoothly and all the relevant questions were resolved and the operation concluded within a few minutes. At this point the bank manager asked my teacher, who was also a client of the bank, why she had not yet opened a certain type of savings account which qualified for advantageous tax breaks. My teacher said that she had not yet thought about it and in fact had problems trying to save in that period, her account being often overdrawn. To my great surprise, however, she concluded by remarking that it was a good idea in any case and asked the clerk to prepare the documentation needed to open the account. Coming out of the bank I asked her why she was intending to open that account, adding that financially speaking it made no sense to place small sums in a savings account which offered a very low interest rate while at the same time paying higher interest on an overdrawn current account. I continued that it would be much more sensible to make use of any savings to reduce the overdraft and only when this was paid off completely to start putting money into the savings account. This was not rocket science, being just plain common sense from an economically rational point of view, but nevertheless it was quite the opposite in the context of the psychology of savings and of expenditure.

My teacher's reply was that I might indeed be right in theory, but in practice she thought and acted along different lines. Basically, she said, the fact of having opened the savings account would be a way of forcing her to save because she wouldn't be able to lay her hands on that money in any case. Sure, paying money into that account would mean her current account would continue to be in the red but, she argued, there was a limit to how far she could go overdrawn and it was better if part of the overdraft was accounted for by savings rather than simply by spending.

If one accepts the idea that problems of self-control are real – in this case relating to the limitation of expenditure – my teacher's strategy displayed a form of rationality. Where the current account represented a sort of open-access area which could be raided without qualms, the savings account was rather like a protected area, inaccessible for the purposes of normal everyday consumption. This represents a further case where the form in which wealth is held has influenced the manner of its exploitation and, once again, where this is the result of a conscious and specific objective, which is that of limiting spending.

7.3 THE PURPOSE OF MONEY

So far we have examined cases where the sources and the allocation of wealth involve violations of the principle of fungibility of money. But the way in which we intend to spend money can also have this effect. More specifically, the manner in which the objective and the context of expenditure are registered and categorized can drastically affect purchasing decisions. Thaler (1980) has remarked that such registration and categorization of expenditure has three basic functions.

The first corresponds to the direct perception and 'labelling' of a specific purchase. Registration takes place when the subject makes a purchase and is aware of and will remember the consequences in terms of expenditure of resources. The second function corresponds to the construction of a clear framework displaying the alternatives available in order to be able to perform calculations of trade-off analysis in a straightforward and effective manner. In Chapter 4 when examining the paradox of choice we saw how the number and the comparability of multiple options needing to be considered in terms of trade-offs can affect our decisions. The framing of these options in a manner considered helpful for the decider can certainly facilitate the act of choosing and thus influence it. The third function of the categorization of choices relates to the application of self-control mechanisms. Expenditure may be deemed worthwhile or otherwise according to how it is categorized. Spending €100 to eat out at the restaurant may be considered excessive if we are simply spending an evening with friends, while the same sum may appear the least we can do if our intention is to express our gratitude to someone who has just done us a big favour.

Let us begin with the process of registration. In many cases small sums of everyday expenditure may not be registered at all. These may be so insignificant that it is not worth the trouble of registering them, even from a hedonistic point of view. The sales and marketing strategies for many products are based on exactly this hedonistic insignificance. Classic advertising messages of the type 'It costs only 10 cents a day' are designed to exploit this factor. The absence of registration means that such expenditure will be virtually ignored, where if collected together to make an annual expenditure of €36, for example, it could take on a certain significance and be blocked as exceeding a certain threshold level. A number of publicity campaigns in the telecoms field act on this type of psychological mechanism, underlining the small daily or weekly sums required to send an SMS, get a flat-rate fixed line deal or a deal for a certain number of gigabytes of data traffic. The opposite situation is when a number of small expenses are lumped together in order to make them less attractive. An example is the type of ads which invite us to add up our daily expenditure on cigarettes in order to make us realize what else we could buy with the accumulated sum, for example a holiday in the Caribbean or a new sofa for the living room.

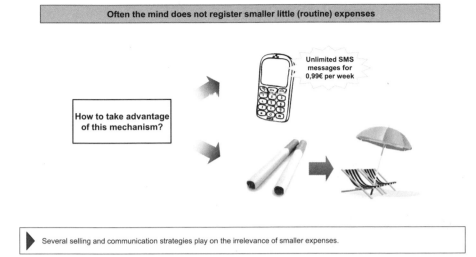

Often the mind does not register smaller little (routine) expenses

How to take advantage of this mechanism?

Unlimited SMS messages for 0,99€ per week

Several selling and communication strategies play on the irrelevance of smaller expenses.

Figure 7.2 Mental accounting: which expenses do I remember and which do I forget?

Money spent on other goods which we perceive as similar, alternative or complementary can also play an important role. If, for example, we have already bought four jazz CDs this month, our decision on whether or not to buy another one will be influenced by our attitude to overall expenditure for CDs in the month, not to mention other similar products such as MP3 downloads, books or DVDs. A further consideration will relate to our preferences and budget constraints following the purchase of the first 4 CDs. But over and above any consideration of affordability or utility in relation to a specific concrete example, the fact of assigning the fifth CD still to be bought to a category such as 'leisure and cultural development' could radically increase our willingness to buy, while its categorization under 'more money spent on music this month' would have the opposite effect.

By selecting certain strategies of registration and of categorization of expenditure, the consumer is at last able to bring into play mechanisms of self-control. We have seen previously that the allocation of money in certain forms, such as shares paying regular dividends, the Christmas savings scheme or the opening of a savings account despite an overdrawn current account, can strongly influence our spending behaviour, helping us to save in situations where we are worried that our will-power will not be enough.

The systematic registration of expenditure can help us in a somewhat similar way insofar as it will bring into focus the amount and the purpose of our spending so that any imbalances between our spending intentions and our actions will appear in a more glaring light. In the same way, categorization will help us to formulate clear rules of expenditure and to make sure that we are following them. For example, if I don't know how monies earmarked for leisure activities are spent it becomes difficult then to know if I am spending too much on CDs and hence to place a limit whereby I cannot buy more than two of them per month. On the basis of categories of expenditure we can thus lay down simple and clear rules of conduct. These will act to facilitate self-control inasmuch as any violation will be immediately apparent and will induce feelings of regret and reduced self-respect which should then serve to correct our behaviour.

CHAPTER 8

ULYSSES, THE SIRENS AND THE CHALLENGE OF SELF CONTROL

In Chapter 4 on the subject of the paradox of choice we saw how the assumptions of economic theory with regard to the desirability of a large number of options for choice are not always valid. Sometimes increasing the number of options can have a negative effect for the decider while certain types of constraint can be beneficial. There is another category of situations where limiting the number of choices available leads to an advantage for the decider. These are ones where problems of self-control are involved. A rational consumer, according to economic theory, assesses the options available in the light of his preferences, which are supposed to be consistent over time. As a result of a positive discount function, a positive pay-off generally has a higher value today than it would tomorrow. However, whether or not a given option A today is preferable to an alternative option B tomorrow depends on the absolute difference in values between the two options as well naturally as on the extent of the decider's preference for the present compared to the future. This preference once decided is supposed to remain stable over time and thus to determine the choices which are then in fact made. On the basis of this logic, if I prefer €200 in a month and a day to €100 in a month exactly, then I should prefer €200 tomorrow to €100 today. The basic assumption is that the discount function will remain stable over time and will not vary with the time-lag preceding the pay-off.

8.1 TEMPORAL INCONSISTENCY

As Loewenstein and Elster (1992) showed in their collection of articles on this topic, there are numerous empirical contexts which show that often this temporal consistency does not apply in practice. Preferences can change over time, sometimes radically. This can obviously be a highly rational mechanism in cases where the change reflects the arrival of fresh information which will lead to a new assessment of the situation, thus modifying our judgement together with our practical intentions relating to a given option. However, there are also cases where this change is not due to our having changed our mind but simply to the fact that we are not able to put our intentions into practice. In these cases we speak in terms of lack of self-control.

Problems of self-control arise in situations where at moment A the individual plans to act in a certain manner at moment B, only to act in a different manner when moment B arrives and then to regret it at moment C, wishing he had conformed to his original plan of moment A. If this change in preferences over time is not motivated by the arrival of new information which cause him to change his mind (twice) but simply by the fact of having lacked the willpower to put his original plan into effect, then that individual can be characterized as having a problem of self-control.

The interesting aspect of this situation is not so much the change in preferences – which could in fact be determined by the arrival of new information – but rather the activation of compulsive mechanisms which cause present preferences to prevail over anticipated future ones. It is the very existence and the application of these mechanisms of self-control which justify the hypothesis that the decider's preferences are not modified by the arrival of new information. It seems rather to be a lack of willpower which causes the decider to depart from his original preference, only to regret it later. It is precisely because he fears not to be able to abide by his intended plan at the decisive moment and expects to regret this at a later time that the agent brings into play mechanisms which will oblige him to act in accordance with his original intentions.

8.2 CONTROLLING SELF-CONTROL

The problem of self-control and the corresponding activation of mechanisms which limit our ability to choose is thus associated with contexts characterized by a time factor – in other words a clear divide between the phases of planning, implementation, results and assessment of an action – together with a volitional factor, in the sense that the agent is faced with genuine alternative options and can thus freely decide on a course of action.

The myth of Ulysses and the Sirens is an emblematic example of this type of situation. The Homeric hero has himself tied to the mast of the ship by the crew in order to be sure he can avoid falling under the enchantment of the Sirens' song. The reason he elects to adopt this stratagem is that he foresees the danger of throwing himself into the sea at the sound of their song with the attendant risk of never making it back to Ithaca. To avoid this danger he deliberately decides to preclude certain possible courses of action. More specifically, he avoids the possibility of physical movement. In actual fact, by having himself tied to the mast, Ulysses ensures that he will be true to himself over time. In a prior moment of lucidity he sets himself up to be able to fulfil his anticipated wish following the moment of temptation, i.e. to continue his journey towards home. Basically, in order to obey the Ulysses of the far-removed future, the Ulysses of the present moment obliges himself to disobey the expected impulse of the Ulysses who will appear in the near future. He obliges himself *today* to do *tomorrow* what *the day after tomorrow* he will wish to have done *yesterday* (Fig. 8.1).

Mechanisms designed to limit options of choice can also have an interpersonal function. Although Ulysses' stratagem was intended to help him be true to his own intentions over time, the elimination of certain options can also help to regulate relations with others. A notable example of this phenomenon is the 'doomsday device', the automatic military response mechanism much debated during the Cold War and wonderfully illustrated in Stanley Kubrick's *Doctor Strangelove*. The principle is that any nuclear attack will automatically trigger an immediate retaliation on an equal or greater scale. To the extent that the party hoping to avoid war commits itself to react by inflicting unsustainable losses on a potential aggressor, this in theory may convince an enemy not to attack in the first place. However, in view of the fact that any such retaliation would incur unsustainable losses on both sides, there must be some mechanism which gives credibility to the threat. This factor explains the two fundamental characteristics of the doomsday device, namely that it is automatic, not requiring an active choice to trigger it, and that it is irrevocable because it cannot be recalled. In the presence of these two elements (at least in the perceptions of the parties involved), neither side will be inclined to initiate an attack. The very certainty of retaliation avoids the need for a retaliation. Unlike the case of Ulysses, the self-limitation or circumscription of one's own range of actions in this case takes on a social function. The fact of

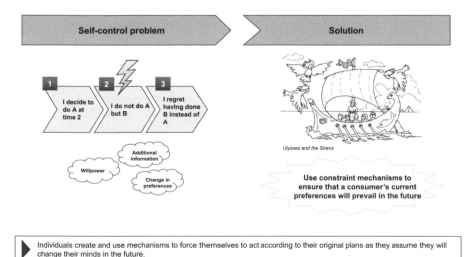

Individuals create and use mechanisms to force themselves to act according to their original plans as they assume they will change their minds in the future.

Figure 8.1   Self-control: what if I can't succeed in restraining myself?

obliging oneself to act in such a manner as to make specific threats or intentions credible means that the agent can determine or influence the actions of others, thus making possible a regulation of relations between the different parties, even in situations of conflict.

8.3 THE MARKET OF SELF-CONTROL

Let us now turn to the business applications of these self-control mechanisms. On the subject of mental accounting in Chapter 7 we described the self-control motivation behind the Christmas club savings scheme. The publicity on the West Virginia Central Credit Union website says:

> *Why wait until it's time to do your Christmas shopping to find out there isn't enough money to make something special. Start a Christmas club account at WV Central Credit Union now and save a little every payday. If you begin the year by saving $20 every two weeks you would have $480 plus dividends disbursed to you by the middle of October for your Christmas purchases.*

Christmas club accounts are a classic example of a self-control mechanism. Of his own free will, the would-be saver opens the savings account. This will reduce his scope for spending money over the course of the year, thus activating the self-control mechanism. The reason for this is that by opening the account the saver commits himself contractually to pay a certain proportion of his income into the account and not to withdraw it until the period immediately before Christmas. In exchange, however, he will be offered an interest rate which is no more or even lower than what would be offered on a normal deposit account.

This is exactly why the motivation for opening this type of account cannot be explained in economic terms. Indeed, Christmas savings club schemes constitute a far from attractive proposition from a financial point of view. They offer neither liquidity nor a good return. Yet the former is precisely what makes them interesting. They help the saver to try and limit the amount of money wasted or sacrificed to small everyday temptations. By channelling a part of earnings into a safe haven, whence it will be difficult to extract the money prematurely, the saver shields himself from any risk of a change of heart, a risk which will rear its ugly head repeatedly during each shopping trip from here to Christmas.

Another very intelligently configured savings product is the so-called SMarT, standing for the Save More Tomorrow scheme. Conceived by Thaler and implemented by major finance houses such as Fidelity and Vanguard, the basic idea is for savers to commit themselves from the moment of starting a job to the payment of an increasing quota of their salary into a savings plan. Long before the moment when the sacrifice needed for saving becomes apparent, the employee signs a contract which provides for the automatic deduction of sums from his pay into the scheme. Starting from small amounts which are relatively 'painless', the sums increase over time in line with salary increases obtained by the employee. Essentially the net salary in the employee's pocket remains constant because any rises are almost entirely subsumed by increases in payments into the fund.

At least three characteristics of this product render it particularly attractive from the point of view of the psychology of choice. First of all is the 'commitment effect'. By signing a contract committing him to pay in a monthly sum, the saver is attaching an added cost to not saving. To be released from this contract will involve bureaucratic formalities, financial penalties and probably also fiscal drawbacks. With its system of automatized deposits, the scheme also provides an antidote to laziness and inertia. The saver need do absolutely nothing, no online procedure, no visits to his branch, no calls to his financial adviser, in order to save. The system runs itself, automatically, deducting regular sums from the current account where the salary is paid. Last but not least, by matching the increases in the investment to increases in salary, it avoids an evident and clearly perceptible loss, because the net disposable income of the saver remains the same in nominal terms, avoiding the unpleasant sensation of losing out or doing without something. Of course, in the medium term inflation could produce an equivalent sensation in terms of perceived financial well-being, but this will probably be attributed to more generalized factors and not specifically to the savings scheme.

A third interesting example of self-control mechanisms relates to running-companions who can be seen in city parks at all times of day and night. Jogging in pairs is not necessarily a good idea. Firstly, it might not be easy to find a companion with similar levels of fitness who therefore would not act as a brake or accelerator on our natural rhythm of running. To be able to chat while running may be agreeable and relaxing, but is not necessarily a good idea, for example in cold weather or for those who are not in good shape. Running with others nevertheless is very popular and this is probably not due only to feelings of fellowship.

An equally convincing explanation – indeed more so for the present author as well as for many of his friends and colleagues – is that running in itself is not actually very much fun and therefore it is necessary to find other compelling inducements. The so-called happy hormones which are released in the wake of a good training session undoubtedly provide a positive factor. However, they are felt after, not during, the session and therefore offer a motivation only for those athletes who are able to anticipate or gain a foretaste of them beforehand.

The fitness factor derived from running certainly also plays a fundamental role in its attraction. Whether or not one finds it fun, a good run is beneficial for the health if undertaken sufficiently regularly. But here too the time shift factor must be taken into account. It is true that running does you good, but only in the longer term. First you have to overcome your laziness and get out of your warm bed an hour early in order to tire yourself out running for 45 minutes, in all probability in the rain, and this effect is felt immediately. The immediacy of the associated cost, or sacrifice, together with the remoteness of the benefits makes it more difficult to put your good intentions into practice on a regular and sufficient basis.

Given that would-be runners consider these good intentions highly desirable, however, they activate certain mechanisms which are designed to render the 'lazy' alternative much less attractive. By combining running with a commitment taken with another person to meet at an agreed time and place, they are adding the observance of important social norms such as punctuality and reliability to the mix together with the runner's 'high' and the long-term health considerations mentioned above. Staying at home now means not only letting yourself down, but also shows discourtesy or lack of respect towards the companion. This puts in place a mechanism of self-control which helps us to put into practice our good intentions.

The market has also showed its understanding of these mechanisms by offering very similar ideas for promoting self-control. A while ago I decided to hire a personal trainer to accompany me on runs once or twice a week. In seeking a suitable person I took into account, aside from sporting qualifications, also the need for an agreeable character with whom I could envisage spending time in a relaxed manner. My true need was in fact for a 'sparring partner' who would call or send an SMS at regular intervals to propose going for a run and, once the appointment had been fixed, would duly come and ring on the doorbell, obliging me to get changed and ready for action.

In objective terms, this person was a freelancer paid to come running with me so that there were no particular ties of friendship or etiquette to follow which would oblige me to go jogging even at times when I had no desire to do so. But the idea of making him come all the way to my house only to send him away without having done the training as agreed would in any case not be acceptable in terms of respect for another person's work and commitment, not to mention the waste of money in that I would have spent a fair amount for nothing. The self-control mechanism which came into play was thus not too dissimilar to what would have been the case had it been a friend.

Through the device of the personal trainer the market for sports activities had in any case offered me greater flexibility and enabled me to develop more effective self-control mechanisms. For example, there were many fewer difficulties finding days and times suiting both parties in comparison with the situation when I used to go running with a fellow-student at the time of my doctorate. By eliminating the excuse of saying 'I don't go running because I can't find a time which suits both me and my running companion', the number of runs planned together with the number actually undertaken increased considerably.

Many products and services exist whose main aim is to assist the purchaser in developing improved self-control. Specialized diet clinics or those helping people to stop smoking as well as products and medicines designed for the same end are classic examples of this. Here too it is a matter of activating mechanisms – whether chemical, physical or social, i.e. based on rules of behaviour – which, once activated, can nudge our behaviour patterns in the direction of objectives which are consciously desired but which may be unattainable due to lack of willpower.

The purpose of the self-control mechanism is thus precisely that of reducing the willpower required to implement our actions, replacing it with a new conception of the way the choice is framed. Many products designed to help us diet, for example, do so by reducing the appetite, thus bringing the temptation to overeat under greater control. In the case of clinics, as for physical activity or the use of pharmaceuticals, the strategy is simply to avoid temptation by serving very frugal meals or not offering foodstuffs which are incompatible with dieting. In this manner, for real food-lovers or for those with problems of food-dependency or obsessions, the fact of deciding to purchase appetite-reducing products or to enrol at a clinic implies activating mechanisms for self-control. Knowing themselves unable to lose weight in a normal manner by simply eating less and thus implementing their decisions on a day-by-day basis by plain acts of willpower, these people rely on this type of 'lever' acting on willpower through these mechanisms of self-control.

Mechanisms of a directly physical type such as pharmaceuticals are thus joined by others of a more psychological nature such as a commitment towards a friend or a personal trainer. This latter type characterizes such interesting Internet services as Tweet Spending or Stich. The idea portals such as these have in common is to make use of the element of 'social standing' to induce the decider to follow a certain plan of action formulated in advance. Conscious of the difficulty of following a desired course of action, the idea is to announce it beforehand, committing oneself in the eyes of a vast public of onlookers to do exactly what is announced. The idea here is that, once the announcement is made, the incentive to match actions to words will be magnified accordingly. The price for not doing so will no longer be the simple failure to achieve an objective in itself (for example, not finishing reading the documentation regarding a new insurance policy because of not having devoted enough time to it) but also the fact of displaying to others one's own incapacity to deliver what was promised, engaging in idle talk or not being a completely reliable person who is in command of his actions. This would naturally lead to an additional cost to our reputation which could have an even greater counteractive force. Not to finish reading through the documentation is possibly not so serious, but to demonstrate one's inability to do so to friends and colleagues could be much more so.

The fact of communicating our intentions in advance and staking our reputation on their implementation can thus redefine the importance of these intentions and can stimulate us to put them into practice. Twitter and Stich provide up-to-date and innovative public platforms for the activation of self-control mechanisms which in themselves are nothing new. Peer pressure has in fact always had a very strong influence on behaviour. The deliberate communication of specific intentions in regard to an action where such communication is not required means deliberately incurring this type of pressure in order to guide one's behaviour. This therefore constitutes a self-control mechanism, because it increases the possible benefits of effective performance of our intentions by extending to others the awareness of our having done as we intended. For the same reason it also increases the costs because a failure to achieve what we intended will involve a cost to our reputation that very often we are unwilling to bear.

Passbook loans are another financial product with a self-control function. In this case, however, the saver's liquidity is increased rather than diminished as in the case of the Christmas savings account. The passbook loan essentially makes it possible to obtain a loan secured by assets such as stocks and bonds held in a portfolio. It serves basically to give increased access to credit while avoiding the need to sell off holdings. From a purely financial point of view, it does not necessarily constitute an option which is advantageous for the saver. This is because in cases where the holdings offer a lower return than the interest payable on the loan, it makes much more sense to sell holdings to the value of the sum to be borrowed. Furthermore, even if the expected return on holdings were higher than the interest rate on the loan, it would still not necessarily make economic sense. This is because where the interest payable on the loan corresponds to an identifiable cost, in the case of the return on holdings we need to factor in the risk factor associated with that type of investment.

In speaking of mental accounting in Chapter 7, we saw, however, that the manner in which we register and categorize financial transactions does not necessarily conform to the dictates of rational economics as based on perfect cognitive and volitional conditions. Insofar as the passbook loan imposes periodic and regular repayments of a certain quota of the loan, it also involves a self-control mechanism encouraging saving and the restoration of the original assets. A straightforward sale of a part of one's investment portfolio, on the other hand, would incur the danger of abandoning oneself to the availability of the short-term liquidity, while remaining unable to make the sacrifices needed to build up one's financial assets over time.

I remember very well a discussion with my father a long time ago concerning the family's financial situation. Outlining to us children how the savings were organized, he explained that we had a certain number of property assets together with a slightly larger amount invested in funds. On top of this was an outstanding bank mortgage which amounted to around 50 per cent of the value of the investment funds. Seeing an opportunity of paying down the mortgage by selling funds, I asked my father why he did not do this. The answer was essentially a mini-lesson in mental accounting. Although I do not remember the exact words, the gist was as follows:

> *Well, Enrico, if one month I spend too much and I don't have enough to pay the instalment on the mortgage, you can be sure I'll receive a call from the bank manager asking me what's going on. If I don't pay for two consecutive months, the phone calls will start to get more insistent and probably more unfriendly too. If I carried on like this for a longer period, instead of phone calls I would start to receive injunctions for payment. I can't bear that type of phone conversation or injunctions. The desire to avoid them helps me to control my spending, and yours too. If I sell some of the funds, the bank manager might enquire why. But once the decision is taken that's it, no one will call me to propose I buy them back. At the end of the day, it's my money. The bank will call me to get its own money back, not mine.*[1]

The decision was therefore between whether to oblige oneself, with a mortgage, to save a certain amount every month in order to pay the monthly instalment, or to leave oneself free to reacquire some funds in the event that one had money left over for that month. Conscious of the difficulty of saving voluntarily, my father had preferred the first option. From his point of view, the interest payable on the mortgage was not the result of poor financial planning, but simply the price for having a self-control mechanism. This 'lever' was necessary to bring into play the willpower required in order to achieve longer-term objectives and so had to be paid for.

Pricing models in use in many sectors can frequently be used by consumers as instruments of self-control. Essentially this amounts to models involving the need to make advance payments in order to gain access to products or services which, however, the purchaser suspects he will not make use of due to lack of time or willpower. Classic examples include the annual enrolment at the gym, the series of sessions with the physiotherapist, the theatre season ticket or the magazine subscription. In earlier chapters we had examined the fact that such pricing models technically constitute irrecoverable costs and so should influence future decisions only to the extent that they avoid incurring additional costs. If the enrolment fee for the gym is not recoverable, our decision whether or not to go should not be influenced by our having already paid the fee. That money is already spent, lost. If the expected utility derived from going to the gym in terms of health and physical fitness is greater than the expected disutility in terms of the effort required to

---

1   My father is a lucky man, clearly having never met any particularly dynamic relationship managers!

overcome our laziness or to do the exercises, or the possible alternative pursuits to which we could dedicate that time, then we will go. If, however, the disutility exceeds the utility, we will opt for the alternatives.

So much for economic logic. In reality, however, this is not the way we normally reason. To pay the enrolment fee and not to make use of the service is more normally considered a waste, a sort of opportunity lost. With that money we could have gone on holiday or bought a new computer. Since we have now spent the money on it, it is better to go to the gym and make use of it. The fact of paying in full immediately can thus have a self-control function. The consumer knows very well that that payment in the past will influence his future behaviour and reduce or modify his range of options. The regret entailed by not going to fitness training will be all the greater because, in addition to considerations regarding health and personal fitness, additional factors of an economic nature will come into play, pushing us in the same direction. The incentive is greater and this will increase our chances in the short term of acting in accordance with our long-term objectives.

CHAPTER 9

MIND GAMES

Many of our decisions are based on our expectations regarding the probability of certain events. The questions we ask ourselves in relation to the past, the present and the future often arise from our doubt. What is the likelihood that object A belongs to category B or that process A causes event B? If I buy a lottery ticket, what are the chances of winning the jackpot? What influence will the price of oil have on the interest rate of my mortgage? How will the share prices of companies I have invested in perform in over the next five years? If I buy the latest model of Mercedes will I be able to avoid the need for unscheduled repairs in the next three years?

Giving a satisfactory answer to questions like these is not always easy. In theory, we need to analyse a vast quantity of information in order to find the best answers, often encountering gaps in the data available not to speak of limits on the time we have to collect and process this information. Making a positive decision will also involve a considerable cognitive effort, because putting together all the factors will require overcoming the limits of reasoning and calculating power which even the most intelligent people have. Lastly, aside from cases where the event to be determined is limited to a clear and predefined context, we will never be able to assign an objective probability to that event, if for no other reason than the fact that at a certain point we have to stop collecting information and decide. Needless to say, this cut-off point could occur just as we were about to discover the additional information which could completely transform our expectations, which are always by definition subjective.

9.1 STATISTICAL INTUITION

The social sciences, and specifically the theory of rational choice and statistics, have investigated the validity and the consistency of our judgements as applied to situations of uncertainty, such as for example estimates of the frequency and prevalence of particular categories or assessments of the probability of certain events. Yet they have never given consideration to the psychological mechanisms underlying these judgements, which are often influenced or even determined by heuristics, i.e. cognitive procedures which help to simplify the processes of data collection and analysis, allowing us to arrive at a judgement. The purpose of heuristics is to reduce a complex process of assessment conducted in conditions of uncertainty to a simple cognitive operation. An estimation based on a heuristic avoids the need for the extensive, rational and conscious gathering, analysis and assessment of information. Rather, it amounts to a simple intuition based on clear, plain rules which are immediate and often unconscious. Heuristics represent a kind of short cut in the decision-making process and are particularly useful in situations where time or our capacity for memorization and information-processing is limited or where the available information is incomplete. They can be equally useful in situations involving information overload or involving unclear or uncertain information.

In their original study on heuristics, 'Judgment under uncertainty: heuristics and biases', Tversky and Kahneman identified three basic types of heuristic: representativeness, availability and anchoring. Appearing in the journal *Science* in 1974, the study gave birth to an entire current of psychological research which was to radically transform the study and the conception of human capacity for judgement. Their work brought into question the descriptive capacity of the rational choice model under conditions of uncertainty and provided an explanation for cognitive errors of judgement, so superseding alternative approaches deriving from the idea of circumstantial irrationality, in other words relevant in given situations but not systematic.

Representativeness is found in situations where the probability of a phenomenon is considered to increase according to its resemblance to the characteristics of the population it belongs to or to the specifications of the process which generates it. If we describe a job-holder as very reserved, lacking interest in social relations or very attentive to detail, it will be much more probable that people identify him as a librarian than as a manual worker, even though the number of manual workers is far greater than the number of librarians. This is because the description given matches more closely to the typical stereotype of the librarian than to that of the manual worker and is therefore much more representative of this group.

Availability, on the other hand, refers to situations in which the frequency of a category or the probability of an event is assessed by relation to the ease with which we can imagine or remember something similar. When we assess the chances that a baby might succumb to measles, for example, we will be strongly influenced by the fact that one of our children has recently fallen ill with the disease. In the same way, the perceived importance of a particular political issue will depend on the coverage given to it in the newspapers and our consequent ability to remember related news items and commentary.

The *anchoring* heuristic describes situations where the estimate of a given value is performed by reference to starting data which is then adjusted to determine the final value. The starting value can emerge from the formulation and/or the context of the estimate and can strongly influence it, even if it does not necessarily convey information specific to the estimate in question. In concrete terms, the process of correction is typically inadequate, so that different starting values lead to different end-values, which in turn will normally deviate toward the starting value.

Heuristics work. These cognitive tricks can often yield satisfactory results. They do not lead us to the truth, they do not make us sure we will correctly assess situations of uncertainty. But they can help us to approach more closely to what we seek. In general terms it is the case that examples of a phenomenon of greater dimensions or frequency are easier to remember or imagine than examples of phenomena of lesser dimensions or frequency. Phenomena which have a high probability are likewise easier to imagine than those which are highly unlikely. Further, correlations between two events are easier to establish if these typically occur simultaneously and judging divergences from given reference values is normally more productive than making estimations from scratch without any logical criterion.

9.2 MENTAL REPRESENTATIONS

While general useful, heuristics often lead to systematic errors of judgement. Let us take the case of representativeness. As we have seen, this refers to situations where deciders' judgements on the probability of A are based on the extent of A's representativeness of B, or whether A is similar to – i.e. representative of – B. For example, if the colour of a bag I see in the shop window is very similar to what my wife normally likes, I will be inclined to think that that colour will be OK. If the vast majority of comments made by acquaintances about the reliability of a Mercedes are positive, I will tend to consider it very unlikely that I will be required to pay out for repairs in the first three years, and so on. In many cases this type of extension is plain common sense because I am justified in assuming that my friends' comments are based on their own positive experiences in driving a Mercedes. In the same way, it seems justifiable to assume that I recall that my wife likes that colour because she uses it often and moreover she refers to it in enthusiastic terms.

However, in some situations judgements involving intuitions based on representativeness can lead to systematic decision-making errors. These are essentially due to mistaken assessments regarding the probability of an event, mistakes which derive precisely from the fact that we focus excessively on similarities and neglect other kinds of information.

The first fallacy stems from *insensitivity to the frequency* of the event. For example, assessments regarding the probability that a person has a given profession will be strongly influenced by the degree to which the description of the person which is given corresponds to the common stereotype associated with the profession. However, if one profession is much more common than another, then this fact should be taken into account in the assessment. A study by Kahneman and Tversky (1973) on the psychology of predictions, where participants were given descriptions of the personalities of a number of people who were either lawyers or engineers revealed substantial violations of this principle. One group of interviewees was told that 70 per cent of the sample of those described was made up of lawyers, while the other group was told the opposite, i.e. that 70 per cent were engineers and 30 per cent lawyers. When the respondents were given descriptions closely coinciding with stereotypes regarding the two professions – e.g. highly oriented to objective analysis for engineers or possessing highly developed rhetorical skills for lawyers – and then were asked to assess the probabilities of their belonging to one or the other group, the decisive factor in the decision was the correspondence between the description and the group stereotype, while the overall size of the group was almost ignored. Regardless of whether the person described was taken from a group consisting of 70 per cent lawyers or engineers, the assessment of the person's profession depended fundamentally on the fact that the description matched more closely to that of a lawyers or an engineer (Fig. 9.1).

It is interesting to note that the participants made a correct assessment of probabilities when no information regarding the subject's personality was available. This showed that the assessment of the probability of belonging to the group of lawyers or to that of engineers was performed largely in accordance with the

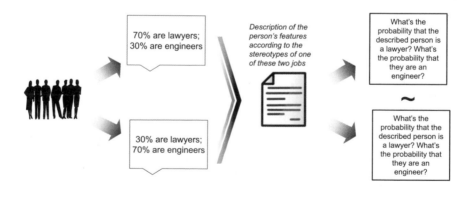

The estimated probability that the described person would be a lawyer or an engineer did not take into account the size of each group in the sample, but only the correspondence of the description to the stereotype

Figure 9.1   Heuristics: what is my job?

rules of statistics, in other words, with the assumption that if a group is composed mostly of lawyers, it will be more probable that a person selected from this group will be a lawyer, while in a group consisting largely of engineers, a person selected at random from the group will be more likely to be an engineer. The availability of relevant information in terms of representativeness as opposed to the complete absence of information thus played a decisive role in the respondents' judgements.

However, when the participants had access to information regarding the personality of the subject in question which was irrelevant in terms of the stereotype associated with their profession, such as their age or marital status, they tended to assign an identical value (0.5) to the probability that the person in question was an engineer or a lawyer, again regardless of the make-up of the group from which the person was drawn. People therefore gave answers which were different – in relation to the initial distribution – when they were given information which was relevant (contrasting with or conforming to the stereotype), when they were given information which was irrelevant (not belonging to the categories established in the stereotype) or when they were given no information.

This cognitive inconsistency can be attributed in part to a general inability on the part of non-specialists (among others) to reason in accordance with the principles of statistics. Statistical reasoning appears counter-intuitive, and thus difficult to manage, from the moment that the complexity exceeds a certain level. In keeping with this is the fact that when no information is given and the lines of reasoning are consequently very simple, results are obtained which conform to statistical theory. However, as soon as the situation is complicated by the need to take other information into consideration – whether it is objectively relevant or not – the ability to reason in a statistically valid way is markedly hindered. Where statistical information is typically remote, abstract and impersonal, the information driving real decisions (particularly judgements of representativeness) tend to be direct, practical and striking. This is why the latter type will frequently trigger dominant thought processes which will prevail over other factors and determine the decision. The question which arises therefore is: in what circumstances does certain information take on emotional rather than rational characteristics and how is the associated representativeness modified so as to increase the influence it will exert on judgement and on choice? As we will further see in relation to the accessibility heuristic, much depends on the way in which information is made available, on how it is represented, and consequently on how easy it is to remember it and make use of it.

Turning to a comparison of the phenomenon of word-of-mouth publicity with statistically valid data available in relation to a given product, let us imagine that we need to assess the purchase of a car on the basis of these two different kinds of information.

On the one hand we have a survey conducted recently by the automobile association regarding the number of breakdowns recorded for the type of car we intend to buy, compiled on the basis of emergency call data from the last 12 months. This survey will be essentially impartial as the organization is independent of the car manufacturers and its central value proposition is to present itself as the driver's 'advocate, supporter and protector' in regard to all motoring-related matters. Further, it can claim a certain statistical validity owing to the number of its members and hence the broad sample they provide.

On the other hand we have the testimony of a taxi driver who has had the model in question for two years and has done almost 200,000 kilometres in it. Where the motoring association survey shows that clutch problems occur very rarely in the first 100,000 kilometres, the taxi driver explains that very soon after putting the car through its annual MOT test his car was out of action for two days due to this type of problem. He tells us with a wealth of details – the trip from the airport to the centre is long – where and how this happened and the problems it caused. Sure enough, when the clutch problem occurred he had been leaving on holiday with his family, it was 4 in the morning, it was raining, the baby was crying and it was cold. He had to call the motoring association's breakdown service (thus enabling them to add another case to their database for the next survey), wait three-quarters of an hour in a lay-by near a tunnel, explain everything to the mechanic, spend the night at a boarding house in an out-of-the-way village and wait for the following day.

In this type of situation it seems clear that our judgement will be disproportionately influenced by the taxi driver's tale. Naturally we will do our best to keep in mind the fact that the data coming from the automobile association has a greater statistical validity and so should carry more weight than the words of the taxi driver. Nevertheless the anecdote bears a much closer resemblance to our preconceptions regarding clutch problems than a bare figure with two decimal places. The driver's story is much more representative of our notions of 'car problems' than any figure, no matter how valid its method of calculation. The single occurrence thus becomes the true indicator of the prevalence of the phenomenon, determining our perception of its frequency (Fig. 9.2)

The nature of the information is not the only determining factor in these circumstances, however. An equally important aspect is the way the information is transmitted. Face-to-face communication seems generally more persuasive than remote and/or impersonal communication, even when the same content is involved. A spoken description of a product is probably more effective, if the person speaking is well-informed and convincing, able to describe features and advantages in a manner more plausible than any brochure. It is not the personal nature of the communication in itself which renders it more effective, but the added impact and immediacy it brings. The notion that a large part of our communicative effectiveness depends not so much on what we say as on how we

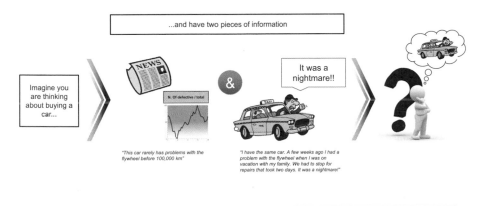

The taxi driver anecdote is more representative of our idea of mechanical problems with the car than any statistical data. So, the (single) episode becomes the true indicator of this phenomenon and determines the perceived prevalence and frequency.

Figure 9.2   Heuristics: what carries more weight?

say it refers to precisely this aspect. This derives from a mixture of tone of voice, facial expression and body language which is difficult to reproduce in a less direct form of communication.

Insensitivity to sample size also causes systematic errors of judgement. Here again, let us see an example. In a survey a group of people was asked to name the probability of the outcome in terms of sequences of heads and tails from a number of tosses of a coin (which was not loaded). The respondents typically considered an alternating sequence of three heads and three tails more probable than a sequence of six tails. From the point of view of statistical logic this constitutes an error of judgement. Given that the coin has no memory, the fact that a given toss yields heads has no bearing whatsoever on the probability of heads reappearing on the next toss. The probability will still be 50 per cent. With an increasing number of tosses the coin will tend to revert to equilibrium, balancing out the number of heads with the number of tails. This means that with an increasing number of tosses, distributions which are perceived as anomalous (i.e. not representative) will not be cancelled out but simply diluted.

The human mind does not appear to follow this reasoning, at least not intuitively and not among non-experts. Rather it appears to note the result of the most recent toss and from this it extrapolates an increased probability that the next toss will yield the opposite result. The cognitive mechanism which gives rise to this error is easily explained by reference to representativeness. A result which is representative of the behaviour of the coin in general terms is expected from an individual occurrence. Regardless of whether it is tossed once or a hundred or a thousand times, we expect that at least in broad terms the number of heads will match the number of tails. A short sequence of alternating heads and tails thus bears a greater resemblance to our expectations of the behaviour of a non-loaded coin than a short sequence of heads or of tails alone. This appears to be the cognitive error which underlies the famous gambler's fallacy, whereby following a long sequence of reds in roulette the gambler will start to expect an increased probability of black coming up. It is as if the roulette wheel, in the same way as the coin, should somehow 'remember' the most recent result and modify its behaviour in order to get back into line with its general pattern.

It is true that many social and physical processes are characterized by this type of self-correcting or feedback mechanism. When for example we speak with a group of experts in order to gain an understanding of a particular empirical phenomenon we anticipate a satisfactory conclusion because we presume that the idiosyncrasies of one expert will be balanced by equal but opposing idiosyncrasies of another expert. In nature itself there are situations where the forces that create a disequilibrium in a particular system will tend to be counterbalanced by opposing forces re-establishing equilibrium. The law of large numbers, which leads us to expect that the numbers of heads and tails or of reds and blacks should somehow balance each other out, does not, however, constitute a mechanism of this type. It simply states that the larger the sample used to study a given population, the more the first will resemble the second. Underlying this similarity, however, there is no causal process of re-equilibrium but simply a statistical description of the real world.

The insensitivity to sample size illustrated in these examples does not presuppose the existence of a causal mechanism re-establishing equilibrium but simply bases itself on the idea that small samples must be representative of the populations they belong to. Some authorities refer in this case to the 'law of small numbers'. People consider that the smaller elements of a process should themselves be representative of the process in its totality, even when the processes involved are random and in no way interconnected. This cognitive error can be witnessed among non-experts in their assessments of the probability of a certain phenomenon, but equally among specialists when, for example, they overestimate the chances that the results of an experiment performed with a small sample group can be applied by extension to the entire population.

In the commercial world there are a number of random processes, not self-referential, which nevertheless are typically assessed according to the law of small numbers. When for example we have a negative experience with a product or with a vendor from a certain company we tend to extend our negative judgement to the company in its entirety. Often, however, the defective product which we experienced simply represents one of the irreducible and inevitable minimum of faulty products which emerge from a particular production line. In the same way, the impatient or ill-mannered salesman is simply the classic isolated example where from time to time even the politest and most professional salesman gets up on the wrong side of the bed one morning and mistreats a client. For the consumer it is difficult to accept that that these are exceptions, or more precisely intrinsic manifestations of a complex statistical phenomenon. On the contrary, the specific negative manifestation of the process tends to be viewed as representative of the process as a whole. The product is defective because it is the sign of bad workmanship and the salesman is bad-mannered because of an insufficiently service-oriented corporate culture.

In this way, the product or the salesman is seen as a problem, a problem which then is seen as widespread precisely because it is presumed to derive from a common cause (bad workmanship or an insufficiently service-oriented culture) and not simply from an oblivious random process. The great care taken by companies in recent years aimed at the reduction of defects all along the value chain (total quality systems, Sigma, etc.) demonstrates a certain awareness of the problem. A mistake made once becomes a mistake made always, and thus very serious. The problem is that this phenomenon is more often of a cognitive than an objective nature. The solution therefore is not just to reduce the number of problems or faults, but to activate mechanisms which will encourage the consumer to perceive these as isolated and anomalous episodes.

Another cognitive problem regarding representativeness is *insensitivity to predictability*. If we examine situations in which people have to make predictions in regard to a particular future phenomenon, such as the profits of a company, the demand for certain goods, the workings of a product or the performance of a particular candidate, in these cases the heuristic of representativeness will likewise be applied.

Let us take the case where the potential future profits of a company we intend to invest in must be calculated. If the description of the company is generally positive, then positive results in terms of margins will be considered more representative than negative ones, in that this is more coherent with the positive picture we have of the company. Internal consistency between the different factors contributing to our assessment will have a strong influence on the degree of confidence, or certitude with which we estimate the probability of a specific future event. If the description of the company consists solely of clearly positive aspects (for example 10 per cent growth in sales over the last five years), then our expectations will be more definite than in situations involving a mixture of aspects which are strongly positive and others which are less so (for example, similar final results but with sales growth fluctuating between 2 per cent and 15 per cent). Another important factor contributing to the certitude of our assessment relates to the nature of the information available. The more marked or pronounced the information, the more we are liable to use it as an indicator, while less well-defined or low-key information will be neglected.

These types of extrapolation or correlation, while sensible and logical in principle, can lead to serious cognitive errors. Very often for example the information used for the assessment of a company's potential is not 'filtered' according to its reliability or appropriateness for the purpose. For example, when an acquaintance whose judgement we respect speaks very highly of an investment made in a certain company, saying that the CEO is a very brilliant person, we will tend to be positively influenced by his words. But what do we know of our acquaintance's knowledge of the specific market the company operates in? And what does he mean by saying a person is brilliant? Charming, hard-working, intelligent? What type of intelligence? Is it relevant for the world of business?

The special importance assigned to the consistency of information can also be problematical. In many cases facts may be highly consistent just because there is a strong correlation between them or even because, essentially, they are redundant. Continuing growth in turnover of 10 per cent may be achieved simply by passively conforming to a market trend, while market share is in fact being lost because the market is growing faster than the company's ability to produce at competitive prices. Fluctuating growth on the other hand may reflect the periodic introduction of innovative products capable of boosting volumes in the short term and then maintaining this in the medium term.

Lastly, extremeness of information can also lead to errors of judgement. A growth rate twice that of the market could for example have been achieved through a very aggressive pricing strategy which may in fact have reduced the company's profits rather than increased them. Instead, growth which matches that of competitors could be a sign of a stable pricing strategy which has brought profitable growth to the entire sector.

Insensitivity to regression can also give rise to errors of judgement. Let us imagine that a group of people have just performed a certain task, such as responding to a general knowledge quiz or doing an IQ test. We could then divide them into two subgroups, consisting of those who performed excellently in the test and those whose results were mediocre. Let us suppose we then repeat the same test or a variant after a short interval of time and that we record the results. Normally it will be observed that the performance of the group who did best first time round will have deteriorated while that of the group who did worse will have improved. This phenomenon is known as regression to the mean, whereby overall results achieved tend to approach more closely to the average with each successive repetition of the performance. Common sense tells us that it is difficult to always perform well or badly, to always get the right answer or the wrong answer. Yet, every time we encounter variations in performance, we tend to seek a causal connection. The athlete was not in perfect condition, the candidate was not well-prepared, the difficulty of the task increased, etc.

One of the most typical errors arising from the misinterpretation of the phenomenon of regression to the mean in terms of causation is the wrongful interpretation of the impact of incentives. This statistical phenomenon can lead to confusion regarding the roles of reward incentives and punitive incentives. Hence a compliment following a good performance may be judged the cause of a bad performance the next time, where the logic of regression to the mean should teach us that maintaining an outstanding level of performance is highly improbable. The number of times my teachers made use of the term 'resting on your laurels' during my childhood escapes me, but it was very frequent. This represented a typical causal interpretation on their part of a situation which was simply a regression to the mean. After having got an excellent result in a test it was much more likely that the next would go badly or at least not as well. Conversely, if a telling-off is seen as leading to a good performance next time, the risk is that we conclude that a negative incentive is effective where in fact here again it is simply a matter of regression to the mean. In a social setting, good behaviour will typically be rewarded with a compliment (a positive incentive) while bad behaviour will attract blame (a negative incentive). This means that it is more probable that behaviour will improve after a punishment or that it will get worse after a reward. However, to assume that negative incentives are more effective than positive ones would be a mistake.

In conclusion, so-called *insensitivity to conjunction* can also be the cause of cognitive errors connected to representativeness. One of the fundamental assumptions of probability theory consists in the fact that the more highly specified the characteristics of an event are, the lower will be the chances of that event coming to pass. It is more probable that a 10 will be turned on a deck of cards than a 10 of hearts. It is more probable that a new tablet will have a nice design than that it will have a nice design and be easy to use. The addition of characteristics to the event in question may, however, increase its resemblance to a prototype we have in mind, thus increasing its subjective probability. In this case the consumer may, for instance, interpret the coexistence of good design and ease of use as more representative of an Apple product than ease of use alone. In this way the existence of a product with both of these characteristics will be seen as more probable than that of a product with only one of them.

In a study involving the assessment of the probability of various scenarios for the final of the 1981 Wimbledon tournament (Tversky and Kahneman 1982) it was considered more likely that Bjorn Borg would lose the first set but win the match than that he would simply lose the first set, regardless of the final result. In another study by Tversky and Kahneman (1982) it was considered more probable that a person described as being very active in the battle for women's rights was a feminist bank employee than that she was simply a bank employee. Both of these examples obviously involve statistical errors, because losing the first set only to win the match is simply one specific eventuality within the set of situations characterized by losing the first set. In the same way, the category of feminist bank employees is simply a sub-set of the category of bank employees. The heuristic of representativeness leads to errors of assessment in these cases precisely because the specification of attributes in relation to a certain phenomenon does no more than render them more familiar and hence more credible. When the person who has just been described to us has a history of civic rights activism, it is easier for us to imagine that her current situation will still somehow be affected by this history, even if the statistical probability is lower.

Such a mechanism is highly interesting in regard to the construction of scenarios with a view to foreseeing the future. The more these are detailed, internally consistent and consequently corresponding to our vision of the world, the more they will be perceived as credible and feasible in comparison to more generic alternatives, notwithstanding the fact that the latter have a greater objective probability. And this leads us to a paradox. The more detailed a description of a product or a service and the more in line with our expectations, the greater the chances that we will consider it accurate and believable. However, the moment the same information which lends credibility goes on to engender expectation, then a greater probability of disappointment will ensue. For example, if on the Internet we see a nice hotel for a week of relaxation, it is easier for us to think of its characteristics in wholly positive or negative terms than in a differentiated and logically structured manner. It is easier to imagine it having good cuisine, nice rooms, great spa facilities and beautiful views than to expect the excellent cuisine to be accompanied by uncleaned rooms. The problem is that the rooms will be judged all the more harshly for the contrast with the generally positive idea we have of the hotel.

9.3 AVAILABILITY AND ANCHORS

Let us now turn to the heuristic of availability. As we have seen, people tend to assess the prevalence of a category or the probability of an event on the basis of the ease with which it can be imagined or brought to mind. For instance, our perception of the probability of catching a particular disease is strongly influenced by the fact of having met someone affected by the same illness or of having encountered numerous references to it. This type of heuristic is termed availability because the frequency or subjective probability of an event is influenced by the ease with which we are able to conceive of this event, in other words the information available in regard to it. As in the case of representativeness, often this is a useful type of cognitive process. It is clear that the more familiar I am with a phenomenon the more I will be able to call it to mind and possibly identify it. Visualizing examples or summoning up associations will therefore be easier, in terms of speed as well as quality, if the phenomenon in question is known or perhaps familiar. Since a phenomenon's familiarity is strongly correlated with its true prevalence, this type of connection can be useful indeed.

However, it is often precisely the ease with which examples, or associations, can be conjured up which leads to systematic errors of judgement. If a member of a category is easier to remember because it is known, then we will tend to consider that category more prevalent than another of equal dimensions but where the single elements are less familiar. If I read a list of words in different languages to a mixed group of listeners, the words in a certain language will tend to be assigned a higher frequency by speakers who speak the language well and who have less difficulty remembering them because they consist not just of sounds, but of meanings. The familiarity of certain words will facilitate their memorization, leading to the increased perceived frequency.

A similar mechanism operates with regard to the vividness with which we recall information. Even the most exhaustive statistics on the frequency of hurricanes will influence our perceptions of the probability of such events less than having witnessed the aftermath with our own eyes. I well recall for example the impression made on me in the summer of 1992 when I returned to Miami, where I was spending a period of study, following the evacuation prompted by Hurricane Andrew. Much of the vegetation at the college had been destroyed and the whole area was absolutely devastated. I probably still have somewhere a photo showing me seated on the uplifted roots of a giant tropical tree, five metres up. The first thing I did on returning home was to ask my parents if we were insured against such events, even though I was well aware of their extreme rarity in northern Italy.

The passage of time since an event is another factor which strongly influences our ability to remember and hence our perception of its statistical frequency. The fact of having just witnessed a bad fall on the ski slopes we will tend to make us more prudent, although this effect will wear off before too long. If we could measure average speeds on the motorway 10 kilometres before and after a nasty accident, we would probably observe a considerable difference, which would gradually diminish, however, as the distance increased.

Errors caused by the ease of imagining examples or associations are also a typical side-effect of the availability heuristic. The more easily we can reconstruct or envisage an example of a given class, the more highly we will rate its frequency or probability. When we need to assess the utility of a new product on the market, in the absence of past experiences to guide us, we will tend to imagine different contexts for its use in order to reflect on its potential usefulness. The easier it is to imagine these, the more we will tend to appreciate the product as being commonly useful.

Obviously the fact that a certain event can be imagined is not necessarily determined by its true prevalence and vice versa. Our expectation of its potential for utilization does not necessarily help us to envisage it. This can lead to serious errors of judgement and perception of the product. The biggest difficulty encountered in selling investment products is that they are not perceived as attractive, precisely because the consumer has problems envisaging their effect in the future. Attempting to assess the annual rate of return on an investment for the period after 2030 often amounts to a purely intellectual exercise. The ability to lead the consumer to vividly anticipate how he will feel in 20 years without that return could transform the perceived attractiveness of the investment.

Turning briefly to the heuristic of anchoring, assessments of specific probabilities or frequencies are frequently made on the basis of a point of departure – the anchor – corrections to which will determine the final value. This can be a very useful cognitive procedure because the point of reference gives us an approximation on which we can base our reasoning and apply corrections. In the absence of this often it could be very difficult to make a reasonable assessment.

In the course of interviews with candidates I sometimes ask them to make an estimate of the size of the population of Italy. It is worth noting that there are three broad types of answer. Some are gross exaggerations (billions of people), some are gross underestimates (a few thousand) and some are approximately correct (a number of millions). Those who provide grossly mistaken estimates – fortunately the minority – also have great difficulties estimating the number of French or German citizens, while those who give a reasonable approximation for the number of Italians are also able to give a sensible estimate in relation to the other countries. Naturally the level of general knowledge may play a certain part in this, whereby estimates are based on a more or less accurate knowledge of the facts. But it is equally plausible that the reasonable estimates for other countries are derived, by a process of extension or correction, from the initial values in regard to Italy. This is because if I start by assuming that the number of Italians is 60 million, it is unreasonable then to say that Germans number either in the billions or in the thousands. Vice versa, if I estimate the number of Italians in the billions, this error will tend to be carried over into my estimate of the number of Germans. Hence it would appear that knowledge or ignorance tend to be contagious, whether in terms of causes – i.e. people's behaviour and attitudes – or of effects – i.e. the cognitive mechanisms for accessing the primary information available.

The use of reference values – anchors – can nevertheless lead to systematic cognitive errors due to the fact that the starting data may be irrelevant or insufficiently corrected. This entails that different estimates are derived from different starting values and may be distorted accordingly. In this regard Kahneman and Tversky (1974) performed an experiment in which participants were asked to specify the percentage of African countries among the members of the United Nations. In the first phase of the experiment a number between 0 and 99 was drawn from a wheel of fortune. After this the respondents were asked if the true figure was greater or lesser than the number drawn. Lastly, they were asked to name the percentage. The initial number drawn from the wheel – which by its nature was purely a matter of chance and therefore statistically irrelevant for the estimate – had a considerable impact on the outcome. The average estimate for the percentage of African nations in the UN made by participants where 10 had been drawn from the wheel was 25 per cent, while for the group where the draw had yielded the number 65 the average estimate was 45 per cent. Currently there are 192 nations belonging to the UN and of these 53 are African, thus amounting to 28 per cent. This shows that the random generation of an initial anchor value can greatly influence the accuracy of estimates. The *anchor effect* is compatible with estimates which can err in either direction (too high or too low) and be insufficiently corrected. The experiment thus shows that completely irrelevant data in terms of content can be transformed into anchors which, once cognitively established, will clearly influence the quality of judgement (Fig. 9.3).

The anchor effect also causes errors in the comparison of dependent and independent events. In many assessment situations, the probabilities of individual independent events are known, while the assessment relates to the overall probability of a given combination. Statistical theory allows for two possibilities in this regard. The first involves the probability that event A will occur in combination with event B. The second is concerned with the probability that either event A or event B will occur. The anchor effect can lead to situations where the single event (the anchor), which constitutes the starting point for the assessment of the overall probability

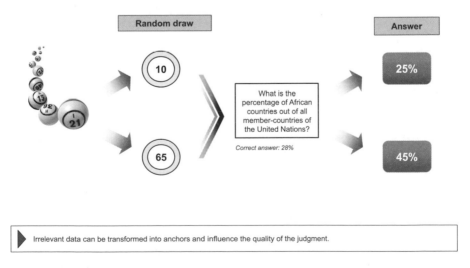

Irrelevant data can be transformed into anchors and influence the quality of the judgment.

Figure 9.3   Heuristics: what are my anchors?

of the sequence of events, has an undue effect on the assessment. For example, in assessing the probability of success of a project consisting of a number phases, each of which has a very high probability, we tend to overestimate the overall chances of success.

Let us suppose that in a marketing campaign it is necessary for a product in development to appeal to clients (75 per cent probability), for supermarkets and shopping centres to agree to place the product in a highly visible position at sales points (75 per cent probability) and for weather conditions to be good during the period of promotion in order to attract a high number of visitors (75 per cent probability). If the process of assessment of the validity of the project begins for example from the estimation of customers' reactions to the product and continues along the other parameters, the anchor effect can lead to excessive weight being given to this first assessment, precisely because the subsequent corrections are insufficient. Certainly, if the probabilities were precisely defined and specified mathematically, it would be easy to perform the calculation, which in this case would be a 42 per cent chance of success ($0.75 \times 0.75 \times 0.75$). If however the cognitive task were to consist in combining less precisely defined probabilities in the context of a less formalized thought process, the tendency to undervalue the combination effect will certainly be greater. In general terms therefore, overall probabilities will be overestimated in the assessment of compound events relating to, e.g., a strategy or a project, to the extent that the initial event (the anchor) is positively assessed.

The non-success of a product on the other hand can be represented as a series of independent events. Sure enough, for the product to fail it is not necessary that all three of the conditions be violated but it is sufficient that only one should be so. In this case, the exact calculation of objective probability could be obtained by the addition of all the possible combinations of events ($0.25 \times 0.25 \times 0.25 + 0.25 \times 0.25 \times 0.75 + \ldots = 58$ per cent) with the exception, naturally, of the one specified above. In this scenario, the anchor effect will determine an underestimate of the overall probability. Indeed, the effect will tend to reduce the upward correction of the assessment of the risk of non-success.

In general terms, it can be said that the anchor effect will tend to cause an underestimate in the assessment of independent events, in other words in passing from the low probability of an isolated event taking place to the high probability of any one of the single events coming to pass.

The assessment of a specific event or state of affairs can be influenced by questions or experiences arising at the moment of the assessment, even if these questions or experiences have no connection to the question to be assessed. The results of a study conducted by Strack, Martin and Schwarz (1988) involving students who were asked two separate questions, the first regarding their overall state of happiness and the second regarding the number of times they had gone out in recent weeks, demonstrated this phenomenon. The order of the questions strongly influenced the assessment of the level of happiness given. The correlation between the level of happiness and the number of times people had gone out was 0.66 for the group who had been asked the question about going out first, while for the second group the correlation was 0. The level of happiness in the former case was thus anchored to the number of times people went out, showing that the students were somehow establishing an inference between one phenomenon and the other. The inference was, however, subordinate to the explicit prior mention of the number of times people went out, which was then transformed into an anchor regarding the level of happiness which had just been brought to the participants' attention through a direct question. Thus it was not the number of times people went out in itself that influenced the level of perceived happiness, but rather whether or not this factor was present in respondents' minds at the moment of assessing their happiness.

In another study a group of students was asked if they would be prepared to pay $10 to listen to some poetry, while another group was offered the same sum as a payment, in the same context. After this both groups were asked how much they would need to be paid or would be prepared to pay to listen to poetry for differing periods of time. Although the students had as yet no idea whether they would find the experience enjoyable or not, their answers were influenced by the initial question. While the first group was willing to pay, the second group expected to be paid. However, in line with the theory of rational choice, they tended to demand or offer a higher price for longer periods of listening. Assuming a random distribution of love for poetry among the students interviewed, the experiment thus demonstrated that the positive or negative monetary value assigned to a given activity shows no necessary correlation with any practical notion of expected utility from that activity. Often we make use of the price associated with the activity as an anchor which constitutes a point of reference from which to derive an estimation of expected value and a consequent willingness to pay.

CONCLUSIONS: SEIZE THE MOMENT

The ideas and experiments presented in this book have an important feature in common which in my view is fundamental for the commercial strategy of a company. This is the role of contingency. The value created by a product and the resulting willingness to spend are strongly influenced by how the choice relating to that product is presented and in turn how it is categorized by the potential customer, regardless of his individual peculiarities. Naturally each of us has preferences which derive from a mixture of factors including our values, attitudes, habits and principles, together making up our personality. The socio-cultural and economic circumstances which have moulded us and which provide the context for our choice will certainly also play a role. Yet, alongside this burden of influencing factors our choices are frequently (co-)determined by the context in which they are taken. It is thus also contingency which guides our decisions and this is a direct consequence of the architecture of the choices we are facing.

Many companies today base themselves on an approach which diverges considerably from this notion. For example, they invest considerable time and money in developing very extensive and sophisticated systems of segmentation, while doing little to understand more precisely which circumstances can have the greatest influence on consumers' purchasing decisions. Starting from the assumption that it is our personal history which determines our decisions, they make every effort to identify those parameters which can help them to define specific consumer profiles and guide them in their approach to individual clients in order to induce them to purchase those products which appear most suitable and attractive. Many different proxies are used in the formulation of this connection and often an attempt is made to coordinate these in order to gain a more detailed and dependable view of the types of customers in question.

By means of a geographical segmentation, for example, the company divides the market into different areas on the basis that consumers' needs and preferences vary in accordance with where they live. The most frequently used variables in this type of segmentation relate to regions, conurbations, population density and climate. A demographic segmentation on the other hand is based on the notion that differences of social profile will determine differences in consumer preferences, making it possible to predict and/or influence buying decisions. Sex, age, income and educational background are the most commonly used variables in this regard. With psychological segmentation consumers' lifestyle is linked to purchasing behaviour, the most common variables being their profession, opinions and interests. Lastly, behavioural segmentation groups individuals on the basis of their knowledge of, attitude to and use of the product, together with their susceptibility to various possible types of marketing methods. Here the most common variables are the type and frequency of use, product loyalty and more generally reactions to the various promotional levers used in the launch and support of the product.

Many critical aspects of this approach to the market and to the client are now widely known, such as the balance between dis-homogeneity and tractability of the various segments, the instability of these over time, their responsiveness to external deciding factors, the limited duration in time of their characteristics, and so on – these are some of the more evident methodological questions. Added to these are organizational and communicative difficulties such as the obtaining of reliable data, the technological complexity of processing this data and the legal sensitivity of its acquisition and use. Even more critical, in my view, is the fundamental problem of the contingent nature of our decisions. As we have seen, individuals act in a certain manner due to the nature of their personality but also to the types of situations in which they find themselves. While the former generate personal motivations which are in some manner taken into account and exploited by segmentation techniques, the latter are at the basis of contextual motivations which are foreign to classical segmentation methods.

In dealing with the loss of rationality in Chapter 1 we examined two recent studies I performed in relation to the deal effect and the anchor effect. In the first of these, the addition of a third option which was clearly less attractive (the credit card sold singly) shifted the preferences for a package composed of current account and credit card as compared to the current account on its own by 22 percentage points, from 59 per cent to 81 per cent. In the second, the reduction in the interest rate from 4 per cent to 3 per cent induced 48 per cent of respondents to invest in a savings account with that rate of interest, while 84 per cent had accepted a rate of 2 per cent when the previous rate offered had been 1 per cent.

The interesting thing about these experiments was not solely that they confirmed the existence of the deal effect and the anchor effect but also their highlighting of the manner in which these effects are valid for all the various segments where they are applied. This means that by analysing the participants' responses in accordance with the typical segmentation criteria, these two effects continue to apply, and apply in a consistent way, for every type of segment. For both men and women, for example, it was much more likely that a package would be accepted if it was compared with the credit card and the current account separately rather than with the current account alone. The fact that the previous deposit account offered a percentage point more or less in interest constituted a variable with a very high explanatory power in terms of a respondent's predicted behaviour regardless of whether the individual had a higher or a lower level of income, and so on.

The question that arises is thus, which is more important, the context or the profile of the individual? Is the make-up of preferences determined more by elements relating to the situation or the segmentation? In general, it is the effects relating to circumstances which carry a greater weight. Of the 24 combinations of segmentation effects and contextual effects tested, 18 appear to be more influenced by the deal effect or by the anchor effect, with a greater difference in preferences identifiable only in 6 cases of segmentation. Even when these differences are weighted for their frequency in absolute terms, context-related effects continue to predominate. This signifies that although sometimes the differences in preferences between segments are slightly larger than those due to context, the latter are much more frequent and pronounced. Context thus plays a more consistent and extensive role in such differences.

Despite these different levels of relevance, the results do not allow us to state that these effects are interchangeable. On the contrary, a combination of the analyses of segmentation and of context appears to be the most effective means to understand the underlying motivations of consumer behaviour. Furthermore, there does not appear to be a strong inverse correlation between context-related and segmentation-related effects. This means that the deal effect and the anchor effect tend to retain a high level of impact regardless of whether the original preferences differ widely within the various segments. The same is true for the inverse relation. Sometimes the differences between the structure of preferences for the various segments are mitigated following the application of the context-related effects, while in other cases they are increased. It is thus possible to affirm that no segments are unaffected by context-related effects and that normally context-related effects are more powerful than segmentation effects, while context-related effects do not necessarily lead to a reduction in the original differences between the various segments.

In my view these discoveries will have a considerable impact on the relation between marketing and sales over the coming years. Companies will have to learn how to measure and exploit these context-related effects through a new approach to the sales process – and more specifically the bargaining phase – which will allow recording and analysis of the effective dynamics of consumer choice. In sectors where sales are made via a face-to-face interaction between the salesman and the consumer, such as automotive, banking, telecoms and PC hardware I believe it will be difficult to prepare individual salespeople to interpret and record the various behavioural aspects which come into play in a negotiation in order to pass these to the marketing section with a view to improving the product range and the types of promotional activity. The 'black box' of the negotiation will have to be opened through the creation of technological instruments able to sustain it through processes of configuration and modification of the offer oriented in real time to the specific choices of the consumer. Such a 'product finder' or 'product configurator' will have the precise task of organizing the various individual elements included in a company's range so as to put together a product appropriate for the individual consumer. The original offer together with possible subsequent modifications and associated value arguments aimed at explaining and sustaining its attractiveness will have to be based on the behavioural mechanisms presented so as to exploit, alongside the product's inherent attractiveness, also that deriving from its representation and framing of alternative choices available. I often make use of the term 'real-time segmentation' in order to express precisely this idea of a concrete accumulation, recording and analysis of the needs of individual clients in the course of the sales process.

The segmentation of the individual customer will thus no longer take place beforehand through the study of his personal characteristics, but will be expanded to include the interaction between these characteristics and the context-related features of the specific bargaining process. The task assigned to marketing will be to prepare in advance an offer relating to a tailored product which can subsequently be modified as appropriate during the sales negotiation and thereafter to equip the sales force with the necessary technological resources to pursue an effective interactive dynamic with the client.

Such instruments will also serve to record the effects of this interaction with the client. It is only through the systematic analysis of the processes obtaining between the salesman and the client that it becomes possible to understand the types and extents of the behavioural mechanisms which come into play for each category of consumer. It is precisely the combination of these two types of information that leads to a significant step forward in the understanding of purchasing patterns. The customer's personality and history will be put together with the context and the process of choice to create a complete picture of the factors involved. It is clear that this approach will entail a partial exchange of roles, with the marketing function determining the sales process more directly while the sales function will have an increased input in the development and configuration of the product.

BIBLIOGRAPHY

Ainslie G. (1986), 'Beyond microeconomics: Conflict among interests in a multiple self as determinant of value', in J. Elster (ed.), *The Multiple Self*, Cambridge, Cambridge University Press, pp. 133–75.

Ainslie G. (1992), *Picoeconomics*, Cambridge, Cambridge University Press.

Ainslie G. (1999), 'The dangers of willpower', in J. Elster and O.-J. Skog (eds), *Getting Hooked: Rationality and Addiction*, Cambridge, Cambridge University Press, pp. 65–92.

Ainslie G. and Haslam N. (1992a), 'Hyperbolic discounting', in G. Loewenstein and J. Elster (eds), *Choice over Time*, New York, Russell Sage Foundation, pp. 57–92.

Ainslie G. and Haslam N. (1992b), 'Self-control', in G. Loewenstein and J. Elster (eds), *Choice over Time*, New York, Russell Sage Foundation, pp. 177–209.

Aricly D. (2008), *Predictably Irrational: The Hidden Forces that Shape Our Decisions*, New York, HarperCollins Publishers.

Ariely D. (2010), *The Upside of Irrationality*, New York, HarperCollins Publishers.

Ariely D., Loewenstein G. and Prelec D. (2003), 'Coherent arbitrariness: Stable demand curves without stable preferences', *The Quarterly Journal of Economics*, 118/1, pp. 73–105.

Ashraf N., Camerer C.F. and Loewenstein G. (2005), 'Adam Smith, behavioral economist', *Journal of Economic Perspectives*, 19/3, pp. 131–45.

Bateman I., Munro A., Rhodes B., Starmer C. and Sugden R. (1997), 'A test of the theory of reference-dependent preferences', *The Quarterly Journal of Economics*, 112/2, pp. 479–506.

Becker G. (1976), *The Economic Approach to Human Behavior*, Chicago, University of Chicago Press.

Benartzi S. and Thaler R.H. (1995), 'Myopic loss aversion and the equity premium puzzle', *The Quarterly Journal of Economics*, 110/1, pp. 73–92.

Camerer C.F. (1998), 'Prospect theory in the wild: Evidence from the field', Working Paper, 1037, California Institute of Technology, Division of the Humanities and Social Sciences.

Camerer C.F. and Loewenstein G. (2003), 'Behavioral economics: Past, present, future', in C.F. Camerer, G. Loewenstein and M. Rabin (eds), *Advances in*

Behavioral Economics, New York and Princeton, Russell Sage Foundation and Princeton University Press, pp. 3–51.

Camerer C.F. and Lovallo D. (1999), 'Overconfidence and excess entry: An experimental approach', *American Economic Review*, 89/1, pp. 306–18.

Camerer C.F., Babcock L., Loewenstein G. and Thaler R.H. (1997), 'Labor supply of New York City cab drivers: One day at a time', *The Quarterly Journal of Economics*, 112/2, pp. 407–41.

Diller H. (2000), *Preispolitik*, Stuttgart Kohlhammer.

Elster J. (1979), *Ulysses and the Sirens: Studies in Rationality and Irrationality*, Cambridge, Cambridge University Press.

Elster J. (1983), *Sour Grapes: Studies in the Subversion of Rationality*, Cambridge, Cambridge University Press, and Paris, Editions de la Maison des Sciences de l'Homme.

Elster J. (1985), 'Sadder but wiser? Rationality and the emotions', *Social Science Information*, 24, pp. 375–406.

Elster J. (1986), 'Introduction', in J. Elster (ed.), *The Multiple Self,* Cambridge, Cambridge University Press, pp. 1–34.

Elster J. (1989a), *Nuts and Bolts for the Social Sciences*, Cambridge, Cambridge University Press.

Elster J. (1989b), *Solomonic Judgements: Studies in the Limitations of Rationality*, Cambridge, Cambridge University Press.

Elster J. (1989c), *The Cement of Society: A Study of Social Order*, Cambridge, Cambridge University Press.

Elster J. (1999a), *Alchemies of the Mind: Rationality and the Emotions*, Cambridge, Cambridge University Press.

Elster J. (1999b), *Strong Feelings: Emotion, Addiction and Human Behavior*, Cambridge, The MIT Press.

Elster J. (2000a), 'Rationality, economy and society', in S. Turner (ed.), *The Cambridge Companion to Weber*, Cambridge, Cambridge University Press, pp. 21–41.

Elster J. (2000b), *Ulysses Unbound*, Cambridge, Cambridge University Press.

Elster J. and Loewenstein G. (1992), 'Utility from memory and anticipation', in G. Loewenstein and J. Elster (eds), *Choice over Time*, New York, Russell Sage Foundation, pp. 213–34.

Fischhoff B. (1991), 'Value elicitation: Is there anything in there?', *American Psychologist*, 46/8, pp. 835–47.

Fogg B.J. (2003), *Persuasive Technology: Using Computers to Change what We Think and Do*, Waltham, Morgan Kaufmann.

Fox C.R. and Tversky A. (1995), 'Ambiguity aversion and comparative ignorance', *The Quarterly Journal of Economics*, 110/3, pp. 585–603.

Frank R.H. (1992), 'Frames of reference and the intertemporal wage profile', in G. Loewenstein and J. Elster (eds), *Choice over Time*, New York, Russell Sage Foundation, pp. 371–82.

Frank R.H. and Hutchens R.M. (1993), 'Wages, seniority, and the demand for rising consumption profiles', *Journal of Economic Behavior and Organization*, 21/3, pp. 251–76.

Frederick S., Loewenstein G. and O'Donoghue T. (2002), 'Time discounting and time preference: A critical review', *Journal of Economic Literature*, 40/2, pp. 351–401.

Gilboa I. and Schmeidler D. (1995), 'Case-based decision theory', *The Quarterly Journal of Economics*, 110/3, pp. 605–39.

Gneezy U. and Rustichini A. (2003), 'Incentives, punishment, and behavior', in C.F. Camerer, G. Loewenstein and M. Rabin (eds), *Advances in Behavioral Economics*, New York and Princeton, Russell Sage Foundation and Princeton University Press, pp. 572–89.

Hsee C.K., Loewenstein G.F., Blount S. and Bazerman M.H. (1999), 'Preference reversals between joint and separate evaluations of options: A review and theoretical analysis', *Psychological Bulletin*, 125/5, pp. 576–90.

Iyengar S.S. and Leeper M.R. (2000), 'When choice is demotivating: Can one desire too much of a good thing?', *Journal of Personality and Social Psychology*, 79/6, pp. 995–1006.

Johnson E.J., Hershey J., Meszaros J. and Kunreuther H. (1993), 'Framing, probability distortions, and insurance decisions', *Journal of Risk and Uncertainty*, 7/1, pp. 35–51.

Kahneman D. (1994), 'New challenges to the rationality assumption', *Journal of Institutional and Theoretical Economics*, 150/1, pp. 18–36.

Kahneman D. (2000a), 'Experienced utility and objective happiness: A moment-based approach', in D. Kahneman and A. Tversky (eds), *Choices, Values and Frames*, New York, Cambridge University Press and the Russell Sage Foundation, pp. 673–92.

Kahneman D. (2000b), 'Evaluation by moments: Past and future', in D. Kahneman and A. Tversky (eds), *Choices, Values and Frames*, New York, Cambridge University Press and the Russell Sage Foundation, pp. 693–708.

Kahneman D. and Tversky A. (1973), 'On the psychology of prediction', *Psychological Review*, 80, pp. 237–51.

Kahneman D. and Tversky A. (1974), 'Judgement under Uncertainty: Heuristics and Bias', *Science*, 185, pp. 1124–30.

Kahneman D. and Tversky A. (1979), 'Prospect theory: An analysis of decision under risk', *Econometrica*, 47/2, pp. 263–91.

Kahneman D. and Tversky A. (1984), 'Choices, values, and frames', *American Psychologist*, 39/4, pp. 341–50.

Kahneman D. and Tversky A. (1995), 'Conflict resolution: A cognitive perspective', in K. Arrow, R.H. Mnookin, L. Ross, A. Tversky and R. Wilson (eds), *Barriers to Conflict Resolution*, New York, Norton, pp. 44–61.

Kahneman D., Knetsch J.L. and Thaler R.H. (1986a), 'Fairness and the assumptions of economics', *Journal of Business*, 59/4, pp. 285–300.

Kahneman D., Knetsch J.L. and Thaler R.H. (1986b), 'Fairness as a contraint on profit seeking: Entitlements in the market', *The American Economic Review*, 76/4, pp. 728–41.

Kahneman D., Knetsch J.L. and Thaler R.H. (1990), 'Experimental tests of the endowment effect and the coase theorem', *Journal of Political Economy*, 98/6, pp. 1325–48.

Kahneman D., Knetsch J.L. and Thaler R.H. (1991), 'Anomalies: The endowment effect, loss aversion, and status quo bias', *Journal of Economic Perspectives*, 5/1, pp. 193–206.

Kahneman D., Ritov I. and Schkade D. (1999), 'Economic preferences or attitude expressions? An analysis of dollar responses to public issues', *Journal of Risk and Uncertainty*, 19/1–3, pp. 203–35.

Karlsson N., Loewenstein G. and McCafferty J. (2004), 'The economics of meaning', *Nordic Journal of Political Economy*, 30/1, pp. 61–75.

Kirsch W. (1988), 'Die handhabung von entscheidungsproblemen. Einführung in die theorie der entscheidungsprozesse', Münchener Schriften zur angewandten Führungslehre.

Kirsch W. (1997a), Wegweiser zur konstruktion einer evolutionären. Theorie der strategischen Führung, Herrsching, Kirsch.

Kirsch W. (1997b), 'Strategisches management: die geplante evolution von unternehmen', Münchener Schriften zur angewandten Führungslehre.

Kirsch W. (1997c), 'Kommunikatives handeln, autopoiese, rationalität', Münchener Schriften zur angewandten Führungslehre.

Kirsch W. (2001), 'Die führung von unternehmen', Münchener Schriften zur angewandten Führungslehre.

Knetsch J.L. (1989), 'The endowment effect and evidence of nonreversible indifference curves', *The American Economic Review*, 79/5, pp. 1277–84.

Laibson D. (1997), 'Golden eggs and hyperbolic discounting', *The Quarterly Journal of Economics*, 112/2, pp. 443–77.

Landsberger M. (1966), 'Windfall income and consumption: Comment', *The American Economic Review*, 56/3, pp. 534–40.

Loewenstein G. (1987), 'Anticipation and the valuation of delayed consumption', *The Economic Journal*, 97/387, pp. 666–84.

Loewenstein G. (1992), 'The fall and rise of psychological explanations in the economics of intertemporal choice', in G. Loewenstein, and J. Elster (eds), *Choice over Time*, New York, Russell Sage Foundation.

Loewenstein G. (1999), 'Experimental economics from the vantage-point of behavioural economics', *The Economic Journal*, 109/453, pp. F25–F34.

Loewenstein G. (2000), 'Willpower: A decision-theorist's perspective', *Law and Philosophy*, 19/1, pp. 51–76.

Loewenstein G. and Adler D. (1995), 'A bias in the prediction of tastes', *The Economic Journal*, 105/431, pp. 929–37.

Loewenstein G. and Elster J. (1992), *Choice over Time*, New York, Russell Sage Foundation Press.

Loewenstein G. and Prelec D. (1992), 'Anomalies in intertemporal choice: evidence and an interpretation', *The Quarterly Journal of Economics*, 107/2, pp. 573–97.

Loewenstein G. and Prelec D. (1993), 'Preferences for sequences of outcomes', *Psychological Review*, 100/1, pp. 91–108,

Loewenstein G. and Thaler R.H. (1989), 'Anomalies: Intertemporal choice', *Journal of Economic Perspectives*, 3/4, pp. 181–93.

Loewenstein G., O'Donoghue T. and Rabin M. (2003), 'Projection bias in predicting future utility', *The Quarterly Journal of Economics*, 118/4, pp. 1209–48.

O'Donoghue T. and Rabin M. (1999), 'Doing it now or later', *The American Economic Review*, 89/1, pp. 103–24.

Payne J.W., Bettman J.R. and Johnson E.J. (1993), *The Adaptive Decision-maker*, New York, Cambridge University Press.

Pink D.H. (2009), *Drive: The Surprising Truth about what Motivates Us*, New York, Riverhead Books.

Prelec D. and Loewenstein G. (1998), 'The red and the black: Mental accounting of savings and debts', *Marketing Science*, 17/1, pp. 4–28.

Rabin M. (1998), 'Psychology and economics', *Journal of Economic Literature*, 36, pp. 11–46.

Rabin M. (2000), 'Diminishing marginal utility of wealth cannot explain risk aversion', Paper, E00–287, Institute of Business and Economic Research, Department of Economics, UCB.

Rabin M. (2001), 'A perspective on psychology and economics', *European Economic Review*, 46, pp. 657–85.

Rifkin J. (2000), *The Age of Access: The New Culture of Hypercapitalism, Where All of Life Is a Paid-For Experience*, Putnam Publishing Group.

Savage L. (1954), *The Foundations of Statistics*, New York, Wiley.

Schelling T.C. (1984a), *Choice and Consequence: Perspectives of an Errant Economist*, Cambridge, Harvard University Press.

Schelling T.C. (1984b), 'The mind as a consuming organ', *American Economics Review*.

Schelling T.C. (1992), 'Self command: A new discipline', in G. Loewenstein, J. Elster (eds), *Choice over Time*, New York, Russell Sage Foundation, pp. 167–77.

Schelling T.C. (1999), *The Strategy of Conflict*, Cambridge, Cambridge University Press.

Schwartz B. (2004), *The Paradox of Choice: Why More is Less*, New York, Harper Perennial.

Sen A. (1973), 'Behaviour and the concept of preference', *Economica*, 40/159, pp. 241–59.

Shafir E., Diamond P. and Tversky A. (1997), 'Money illusion', *The Quarterly Journal of Economics*, 112/2, pp. 341–74.

Shafir E., Simonson I. and Tversky A. (1993), 'Reason-based choice', *Cognition*, 49, pp. 11–36.

Shefrin H.M. and Thaler R.H. (1988), 'The behavioral life-cycle hypothetis', *Economic Inquiry*, 26/4, pp. 609–43.

Shefrin H.M. and Thaler R.H. (1992), 'Mental accounting, saving and self-control', in G. Loewenstein and J. Elster (eds), *Choice over Time*, New York, Russell Sage Foundation, pp. 287–331.

Shefrin H.M. and Thaler R.H. (2003), 'Mental accounting, saving, and self-control', in C.F. Camerer, G. Loewenstein and M. Rabin (eds), *Advances in Behavioral Economics*, pp. 395–428.

Shiller R.J. (2000), *Irrational Exuberance*, Princeton, Princeton University Press.

Shiller R.J. (2008), *The Subprime Solution: How Today's Global Financial Crisis Happened, and What to Do about it*, Princeton, Princeton University Press.

Simon H. (1991), *Preismanagement: probleme und methoden des modernen pricing*, Gabler.

Simon H. (1995), *Preismanagement kompact: probleme und methoden des modernen pricing*, Gabler.

Simon H. and Dolan R.J. (1997), *Profit durch power pricing: strategien aktiver preispolitik*, Campus.

Simon H.A. (1947), *Administrative Behaviour: A Study of Decision-Making Processes in Administrative Organizations*, New York, Free Press.

Simon H.A. (1955), 'A behavioral model of rational choice', *The Quarterly Journal of Economics*, 69/1.

Simon H.A. (1957), *Models of Man*, New York, John Wiley.

Simon H.A. (1986), 'Rationality in psychology and economics', *The Journal of Business*, 59/4, Part 2: The Behavior Foundation of Economic Theory, pp. S209–24.

Simonson I. (1990), 'The effect of purchase quantity and timing on variety seeking behavior', *Journal of Marketing Research*, 27/2, pp. 150–62.

Slovic P. (1991), 'The construction of preference', *American Psychologist*, 50/5, pp. 364–71.

Soman D. (2001), 'Effects of payment mechanism on spending behavior: The role of rehearsal and immediacy of payments', *Journal of Consumer Research*, 27/4, pp. 460–74.

Starmer C. (2000), 'Developments in nonexpected-utility theory: The hunt for a descriptive theory of choice under risk', *Journal of Economic Literature*, 38/2, pp. 332–82.

Stigler G.J. (1961), 'The economics of information', *The Journal of Political Economy*, 69/3, pp. 213–25.

Stigler G.J. and Becker G.S. (1977), 'De gustibus non est disputandum', *American Economic Review*, 67, pp. 76–90.

Strack F., Martin L.L. and Schwarz N. (1988), 'Priming and communication: Social determinants of information use in judgments of life satisfaction', *European Journal of Social Psychology*, 18, pp. 429–42.

Thaler R.H. (1980), 'Toward a positive theory of consumer choice', *Journal of Economic Behavior and Organization*, 1/1, pp. 39–60.

Thaler R.H. (1981), 'Some empirical evidence on dynamic inconsistency', *Economic Letters*, 8/3, pp. 201–207.

Thaler R.H. (1985), 'Mental accounting and consumer choice', *Marketing Science*, 4/3, pp. 199–214.

Thaler R.H. (1986), 'The psychology and economics conference handbook', *Journal of Business*, 59/4, pp. S279–S284.

Thaler R.H. (1987), 'The psychology of choice and the assumptions of economics', in A. Roth (ed.), *Laboratory Experiments in Economics: Six Points of View*, New York, Cambridge University Press.

Thaler R.H. (1992), *The Winner's Curse: Paradoxes and Anomalies of Economic Life*, New York, Free Press.

Thaler R.H. (1999), 'Mental accounting matters', *Journal of Behavioral Decision Making*, 12/3, pp. 183–206.

Thaler R.H. and Johnson E.J. (1990), 'Gambling with the house money and trying to break even: The effects of prior outcomes on risky choice', *Management Science*, 36/6, pp. 643–60.

Thaler R.H. and Shefrin H.M. (1981), 'An economic theory of self-control', *Journal of Political Economy*, 89/2, pp. 392–406.

Thaler R.H. and Sunstein C.R. (2008), *Nudge: Improving Decisions about Heath, Wealth, and Happiness*, New Haven, Yale University Press.

Tversky A. and Griffin D. (1991), 'Endowment and contrast in judgments of wellbeing', in R.J. Zeckhauser (ed.), *Strategy and Choice*, Cambridge, The MIT Press.

Tversky A. and Kahneman D. (1974), 'Judgment under uncertainty: Heuristics and biases', *Science, New Series*, 185/4157, pp. 1124–31.

Tversky A. and Kahneman D. (1981), 'The framing of decisions and the psychology of choice', *Science*, 211/4481, pp. 453–8 e 657–85.

Tversky A. and Kahneman D. (1982), 'Judgments of and by representativeness', in D. Kahneman, P. Slovic and A. Tversky (eds), *Judgments under Uncertainty: Heuristics and Biases*, New York, Cambridge University Press, pp. 84–98.

Tversky A. and Kahneman D. (1986), 'Rational choice and the framing of decisions', *Journal of Business*, 59/4, pp. S251–S278.

Tversky A. and Kahneman D. (1991), 'Loss aversion in riskless choice: A reference development model', *The Quarterly Journal of Economics*, 106/4, pp. 1039–61.

Tversky A. and Kahneman D. (1992), 'Advances in prospect theory: Cumulative representation of uncertainty', *Journal of Risk and Uncertainty*, 5/4, pp. 297–323.

Tversky A. and Shafir E. (1992), 'Choice under conflict: The dynamics of deferred decision', *Psychological Science*, 3, pp. 358–61.

Tversky A. and Simonson I. (1993), 'Context-dependent preferences', *Management Science*, 39/10, pp. 117–85.

Van Boven L., Loewenstein G. and Dunning D. (2003), 'Mispredicting the endowment effect: underestimation of owner's selling prices by buyers' agents', *Journal of Economic Behavior and Organization*, 51/3, pp. 351–65.

Venti S.F. and Wise D.A. (1989), 'Aging, moving, and housing wealth', in D.A. Wise, *The Economics of Aging*, Chicago, University of Chicago Press.

Wilkinson N. (2008), *An Introduction to Behavioral Economics*, Basingstoke, Palgrave Macmillan.

Wuebker G. (1998), P*reisbüendelung*, Gabler.

Wuebker G. and Trevisan E. (2007), *Value Pricing: Come ottimizzare il profitto della banca*, Milano, Il Sole 24 Ore.

INDEX

If you have found this book useful you may be interested in other titles from Gower

Market Orientation:
Transforming Food and Agribusiness
around the Customer
Edited by
Adam Lindgreen, Martin Hingley, David Harness and Paul Custance
Hardback: 978-0-566-09208-4
e-book (ePUB): 978-1-4094-5868-5
e-book (PDF): 978-0-566-09236-7

Shopping 3.0:
Shopping, the Internet or Both?
Cor Molenaar
Hardback: 978-1-4094-1764-4
e-book (ePUB): 978-1-4094-5892-0
e-book (PDF): 978-1-4094-1765-1

Customer Relationship Management:
A Global Perspective
Gerhard Raab, Riad A. Ajami,
Vidyaranya B. Gargeya and G. Jason Goddard
Hardback: 978-0-7546-7156-5
e-book (ePUB): 978-1-4094-6017-6
e-book (PDF): 978-1-4094-0540-5

GOWER

Memorable Customer Experiences:
A Research Anthology
Edited by
Adam Lindgreen, Joëlle Vanhamme and Michael B. Beverland
Hardback: 978-0-566-08868-1
e-book (ePUB): 978-1-4094-5971-2
e-book (PDF): 978-0-566-09207-7

Creating Innovative Products and Services:
The FORTH Innovation Method
Gijs van Wulfen
Hardback: 978-1-4094-1754-5
e-book (ePUB): 978-1-4094-5905-7
e-book (PDF): 978-1-4094-1755-2

The Psychology of Marketing:
Cross-Cultural Perspectives
Gerhard Raab, G. Jason Goddard, Riad
A. Ajami and Alexander Unger
Hardback: 978-0-566-08903-9
e-book (ePUB): 978-1-4094-5944-6
e-book (PDF): 978-0-566-08904-6

Visit **www.gowerpublishing.com** and

- search the entire catalogue of Gower books in print
- order titles online at 10% discount
- take advantage of special offers
- sign up for our monthly e-mail update service
- download free sample chapters from all recent titles
- download or order our catalogue